"A welcome book, full of wise counsel."

Harold Myra, executive chair,
Christianity Today International

"*Damage Control* is nothing less than a thoughtful, well-reasoned presentation that the church in the United States urgently needs to ponder. Through powerful stories and convincing application of Scripture, Dean Merrill perfectly portrays the Christian's role as 'God's ambassador' to the world. What's more, he helps us understand the tools of the ambassador's trade—embracing everything from carefully chosen words to the evidence of God's power. *Damage Control* can make a real difference in how the church impacts a skeptical but needy world."

Wess Stafford, president and CEO,
Compassion International

"Dean Merrill has given us a 'high definition' version of the biblical theme of ambassador. Every person who describes themselves as Christian ought to have to sit silently and listen to Merrill's book read to them. This is a classic lesson in why America is clueless about who Jesus really is. The answer to this dilemma is costly but not expensive. Merrill reminds us this journey starts with acting like the One we say we represent."

Byron D. Klaus, president,
Assemblies of God Theological Seminary,
Springvield, Missouri

Damage Control

Damage Control

HOW TO STOP MAKING JESUS LOOK BAD

DEAN MERRILL

BakerBooks

Grand Rapids, Michigan

Published by Baker Books
a division of Baker Publishing Group
P.O. Box 6287, Grand Rapids, MI 49516-6287
www.bakerbooks.com

Printed in the United States of America

Library of Congress Cataloging-in-Publication Data
Merrill, Dean.
    Damage control : how to stop making Jesus look bad / Dean Merrill.
        p.   cm.
    Includes bibliographical references.
    ISBN 10: 0-8010-6565-8 (pbk.)
    ISBN 978-0-8010-6565-1 (pbk.)
    1. Christian life. I. Title.
BV4501.3.M47 2006
248'.5—dc22   2005026082

Published in association with the literary agency of Mark Sweeney & Associates, 28450 Altessa Way, Suite 201, Bonita Springs, FL 34135.

Contents

Part One

God's Shaky Plan

1

Who, Us?

As you may have noticed, Jesus isn't here anymore. At least not visibly.

If he were, everybody from Jay Leno to Oprah Winfrey to Larry King would be clamoring to have him on their show. He'd be the hottest interview of the season. Can't you just imagine the questions, as the host leans forward in the chair:

"So tell us, Jesus, how's your life going these days?"

"What's going to be the theme of your next tour? What cities have you booked already?"

"What did you think of that last movie about your, uh, rough treatment by the Sanhedrin and Pontius Pilate?"

Studio audiences as well as viewers across the nation would be fascinated. Ratings would soar.

But it won't be happening. Jesus took off (literally) around AD 30 or so. He didn't leave us a cell phone number or an email address. He just disappeared—it was the strangest thing.

Do you know anyone else who started a major enterprise—say, a technology firm or an upscale restaurant chain—and then walked away from it at age thirty-three, when momentum was just starting to roll? Wouldn't you stick around longer to make sure your brainchild stayed on track, met growth projections, and established itself in the cultural marketplace? Maybe after a few decades, when you reached your sixties, you could hand it off to carefully chosen, well-trained successors . . . provided the various important shareholders in the company agreed, that is. Then you could retire in comfort.

Jesus cared passionately about his mission on earth. He had come "to preach good news to the poor . . . to proclaim freedom . . . to release the oppressed" (Luke 4:18) and to embody this work permanently in the form of "my church, and the gates of Hades will not overcome it" (Matt. 16:18). Talk about an ambitious undertaking. This was not to be a cottage sideline. This was a global revolution.

And then he split, leaving Peter and John and Paul, and now you and me, in charge. Whatever gets said or done to advance the effort is up to us. Granted, he still advises us in quiet ways, primarily through his Book. But as far as the public is concerned, we're the spokespeople. We're the "face" of the organization.

Was this a smart thing for Jesus to do? (Not that we would dare to question his divine strategy, but still . . .) Wouldn't ordinary mortals mess things up?

An oft-told fable tries to capture what it must have been like a few hours after the ascension, when the Son of God arrived back in heaven from his earthly excursion. Imagine him briefing the angels: "It was a very long time growing up as a human child and teenager. Then I finally got to start what I'd been sent by the Father to do. I spoke to crowds of people about the coming kingdom of God. I told them God loved them and would forgive them for their offenses against him. I healed the sick. I even raised a few from the dead. I battled with the religious authorities who thought they already knew everything. Some of them got pretty upset—which is what led to my arrest and death. It wasn't pleasant.

"But of course, I wasn't about to stay in that tomb for very long. Soon I came back to the scene, which shocked a lot of people. In the last few weeks I've made it clear that my followers—you know, the disciples—are to carry on my work. They've been commissioned to take the Good News far and wide, not just inside their Jewish culture, but everywhere. In time, the whole world can hear and know the way to enter God's family."

The longer he talks, the more wide-eyed the angels become. Soon, a few of them look puzzled. Finally, an archangel asks, "Uh, Jesus, but what if these followers—'disciples,' I believe you called them—don't follow through? Did I understand you correctly that you've put the whole project in their hands? Everything the Father wants to happen . . . it's all up to them? What if they fail to do your bidding?"

The Son's face grows somber. He is quiet for a moment. Then he softly replies, "I have no other plan."

With that comment, the briefing is over for the day. Everyone leaves the room deep in thought.

Checkup Time

So how are we doing? As the apostle Paul wrote to a group of Christians in Corinth, God "has committed to us the message of reconciliation. We are therefore Christ's ambassadors" (2 Cor. 5:19–20). We are "field reps" for the King of kings. However we represent him in this world is as good as it's going to get.

The cause of Christ is at the mercy of human handling. He deserves, of course, the best advocacy he can get, so that his message of wholeness and eternal life will be heard by those who need it most.

Does Jesus ever look down from heaven these days at the actions of us Christians and say, "What do you think you're doing?! You just made my job 20 percent tougher. Because of this, I'm going to have to employ a different strategy for pushing back the darkness. Everything is going to take longer and will be clumsier. Yes, we can still make progress—but next time, how about thinking about your actions before you proceed?"

Sometimes Jesus's friends are terrific. Other times, they're his own worst enemies. Frederick Buechner writes with astonishment about God being willing "to choose for his holy work in the world . . . lamebrains and misfits and nitpickers and holier-than-thous and stuffed shirts and odd ducks and egomaniacs and milquetoasts and closet sensualists."[1]

How God must cringe sometimes at the ways we who bear his name botch his message, get sidetracked in arguments that don't really matter, and fog our presentations to people who would love to know God but can't make heads or tails of what we're saying.

In my earlier years, when asked on an airplane or at a social function what kind of work I did, I would reply, "I'm a journalist." I was, after all, proud of having earned a master's degree at a well-known journalism school in the Northeast, and I believed wholeheartedly in the value of a free and vigorous press in our democracy. Without the benefit of information and opinion, even uncomfortable opinion, how would voters ever know how to govern the republic?

Well, I still believe all that. But I've stopped calling myself a "journalist." I've found out the hard way that the title irritates people. If I say instead that I'm an "author" or a "writer," it goes down a lot more palatably in America today. Polls by the Pew Research Center for the People and the Press, among others, show a precipitous drop in public regard for the news media. Back in 1985, the percentage of Americans who said news organizations generally "got the facts straight" was 55 percent. Today that number has dropped a full twenty points.

A Gallup Poll in late 2004 measured "honesty and ethical integrity" among twenty professions. Television reporters came in fourteenth, and newspaper reporters fifteenth—far below nurses (in first place), pharmacists and military officers (tied for second), doctors (fourth), police officers (fifth), and clergy (sixth).

Every time a high-profile, Pulitzer Prize–winning reporter gets busted for fabricating his or her story, I cringe. Every time a network news anchor spins a feature to match his or her personal politics, I am embarrassed. As much as I want to defend my chosen profession, I have to admit that it has a disturbing share of incompetence and distortion.

Perhaps you too have found yourself part of a group—professional, ethnic, national, or otherwise—that smudges its reputation, and you feel bad about that. All Americans can remember the sickening feeling in their stomachs when the photos of prisoner abuse at Abu Ghraib prison in Baghdad first appeared. This betrayed everything we believed to be good and decent about ourselves. Syndicated columnist Mona Charen called the pictures "a dagger in the heart of our hopes for Iraq and the wider Middle East. . . . The

Americans who did this are idiots—and one just doesn't know what to say about those who thought it would be a good idea to snap photos."[2] She worried, as we all did, about human nature's way of looking at the deeds of a few people and generalizing to their entire group.

So it is with the group called "Christian." We do not live as individuals. We are a collective body whether we like it or not, and what we do reflects on the entire group, including its leader, Jesus Christ. After all, his name gave birth to ours. We are inseparable in the public mind.

Improving Our Grade

On the other hand, there is a bright side to this discussion. Certain actions by the Christian community deserve genuine applause. Some moves are downright intelligent. We're doing at least some things right.

In this book, I want to look at both sides. I don't plan only to criticize and critique. While I will honestly examine the ways we hurt God's cause without realizing it, I also want to showcase the good things being done by today's ambassadors—the smart moves, the wise endeavors. I hope that, as a result, we can all become more of the solution and less of the problem.

In preparation for my writing, I conducted an informal survey that asked people to name three specific ways Christians were currently representing Christ well. "In other words," I wrote, "what makes you proud to be a Christian?"

The answers were encouraging. Several respondents mentioned ongoing programs of help for the needy, the sick, the disadvantaged. Others spoke about bravery and endurance in the face of persecution, especially among Christians in the developing world. Some said there is less denominational partisanship these days than in the past. Some pointed to efforts to reduce racism in American life. Several talked about the trend among many churches to make the gospel more understandable in today's language, less obscure and "religious."

So we should not give ourselves an F for our efforts on behalf of the cause of Christ. Maybe a C-minus?

If this book can help us raise our grade into even the B range, we'll be making headway. And Jesus will be pleased. That, after all, is the main point, isn't it?

At the end of the day, being a Christian is not really about *my* tradition or *my* subculture. It's not about preserving *my* comfort. It's not about fitting nicely with *my* generation. It's not about safeguarding *my* denomination.

As Max Lucado says with simple eloquence in his book title, *It's Not About Me* at all.

Being a Christian is about Christ. If he is noticed and honored, if his message is listened to, if his influence is expanded, we will have done what "good and faithful servants" were meant to do.

2

Ambassadors at Work

How do Christians today most commonly see themselves in relation to God? What terms and metaphors do they use most often?

"Well, I am a *child* of God," many would say. They view God as the loving Parent and themselves as the dependent son or daughter. This is entirely justified from a scriptural viewpoint.

So would be the response of the person who says, "I'm a *follower* of Christ." The imagery here is that Christ blazes the trail across the landscape, and we try to put our shoes in his footsteps as best we can.

A slightly more religious term would be, "I'm a *disciple*." The term is similar to *follower*, but it also hints at the notion of being shaped by the Lord—of coming under his influence, even discipline. In other words, I'm doing more than just tagging along; I am accepting God's authority in my life to change and improve my being.

Preparing the Way

In the previous chapter, however, we introduced a different self-concept for the believer in Christ: that of *ambassador*. This is not just a passive, deferential role; being an ambassador implies that you will step up to take responsibility for helping the cause that Christ embodies. Many Christians today may, at first, be hesitant to take on such an assignment.

The trouble is, it is our job whether we wish for it or not. Those outside the faith view us in this light automatically. We are assumed to be agents of Christ, representatives of his message, and exhibits of his grace.

The passage from 2 Corinthians 5 assumes the same thing. "God . . . reconciled us to himself through Christ and gave us the ministry of reconciliation. . . . We are therefore Christ's ambassadors, as though God were making his appeal through us. We implore you on Christ's behalf: Be reconciled to God" (vv. 18–20). Like an envoy who works in the diplomatic corps as part of the State Department, we represent God's interests in a certain country. What is that country? The territory where we currently live. It is not our true home forever, but it is our place for the time being.

We are not unlike John the Baptist, sent to "prepare the way for the Lord, [and] make straight paths for him" (Matt. 3:3). His mission was to enable Jesus's forward progress in this world. The more Jesus eventually accomplished, the more John could feel affirmed for his efforts. He was Jesus's "front man," the emissary to focus public attention on the Messiah and show him in the best possible light.

David K. E. Bruce was one of America's premier ambassadors for some three decades, serving both Democratic and Republican administrations. His first assignment was in Paris, where he arrived at the embassy in May 1949. The brutal effects of World War II were not yet erased, and France was still in need of American aid via the Marshall Plan, an enterprise for which Bruce had already labored energetically in his previous posts.

His biographer explains the tricky undercurrents Bruce had to navigate:

> Franco-American relations resembled an edgy friendship. Many in France feared the intrusion of American popular culture, an alien presence trundled into La Belle France in the Trojan horse of Marshall aid. . . . Those rows of big, black American cars with diplomatic license plates parked every day on the Place de la Concorde lent credence to the alarmists. Of all the nations aligned with America, France most strongly resented the subordinating consequences of World War II. In the words of long-time expatriate Janet Flanner, the nation "talks like a spoiled old beauty who still wants her hand kissed in admiration." The more it relied on American aid, the more unhappy the relations.[1]

Bruce, a consummate Virginia gentleman and peacemaker, had his hands full when the Coca-Cola company announced plans to hang a gigantic red sign on the Eiffel Tower. "The thought of a neon sign flashing its obnoxious American message across the night sky was enough to induce fits in Parisians,"[2] who after all viewed themselves connoisseurs of far better beverages. Bruce didn't want to work against the interests of his home country's major soft-drink manufacturer, which was after all simply trying to expand its market. But he knew that if the French got upset and banned the advertising outright, it would set U.S. Congressmen grumbling the next time an appropriations bill for the Marshall Plan came up for debate. He managed, in his smooth and congenial way, to coax Coca-Cola toward a different form of promotion in the City of Light.

That is the ambassadorial challenge: keep two vastly different worldviews from taking punches at each other. It is remarkably similar to the spiritual world, in which heaven (our true home) thinks one way, and the prevailing opinion here on earth is quite another. Heaven has the power to overwhelm the provincial, self-absorbed opinions and prejudices of earth, of course. But it has chosen to employ a diplomatic corps (you and me) to live in the midst of human society and communicate what the other side is really saying.

What God wants to see happen in the world is all too often viewed with revulsion and disgust by people here in our world. They are not open to God's ideas in the least . . . until we come along and show the benefits they may not have previously seen. We are doing what 2 Corinthians 5 calls "reconciling."

A Gap to Be Bridged

Sometimes the issue is not really one of substance but simply style. During the 1960s, David K. E. Bruce was the U.S. ambassador to Great Britain. The two countries' leaders could hardly have been more opposite. On the one side was Prime Minister Harold Wilson, educated at Oxford, "a cautious master of obfuscation, adept at making ambiguous public statements to serve his political aims," Bruce wrote in his diary. On the other side was the tall, rough-and-rugged

Texan in a cowboy hat, Lyndon B. Johnson, "a great black leopard, magnificent, dangerous if cornered," as Bruce put it. Talk about an odd couple.

Bruce took on the dicey job of keeping these two on friendly terms. The U.S. and the U.K. had been staunch allies through two world wars, of course, and now in the midst of the Cold War they needed each other as much as ever. He could not let petty misunderstandings derail the two strongest members of the North Atlantic Treaty Organization.

Johnson could be shockingly blunt, of course, and "after a particularly ribald presidential explosion, Bruce averted a serious rupture by persuading the prime minister to communicate . . . by teletype rather than telephone. Johnson habitually picked up the phone at odd hours when he wanted to put lesser mortals on the spot but resented anyone trying the same trick on him."[3]

Once again, the strategy of building bridges, not letting molehills turn into mountains, and staying calm in the midst of rhetorical flurry proved invaluable. What mattered most was the cause of transatlantic partnership, not who won which argument.

In our case, even more than geopolitical harmony is at stake. This is a matter of heaven reaching out toward earth, wanting to rescue it from eternal disaster. And earth, pigheadedly, is not sure it wants to be rescued. It kind of likes the bright lights and seductive sounds of the broad road that leads to destruction. Not the destination, mind you, but the pleasure of the trip en route.

Ambassadors such as you and I must come alongside and say, "Let's talk about how this trip is going. . . ."

When self-obsessed travelers say, "Why would God ever say such-and-such? That's ridiculous," we reply, "Well, let me walk you through his thinking on that topic. Here's the background. . . ." With every new event, every complication, we exercise spiritual diplomacy. We are "always . . . prepared to give an answer to everyone who asks [us] to give the reason for the hope that [we] have"—and we "do this with gentleness and respect" (1 Peter 3:15).

This obviously entails much preparation and consultation with the heavenly "capitol." Just as today's ambassadors are constantly communicating with their superiors back home, sending encrypted emails on a daily basis, then coming into their offices early the next morning to read what has arrived overnight in order to be ready for the day's challenges . . . so we cannot shortcut our need for discussion with God. After all, the message is not ours but his. Whenever we try to guess what he might say without knowing for sure, we run the risk of embarrassing everyone.

Frequently an ambassador leaves his or her post temporarily to go back home, "recalled for consultation," as the phrase goes. The ambassador sits down face-to-face with the president or the secretary of state, perhaps the National Security Council or the joint chiefs of staff at the Pentagon, to work through current issues and make sure everybody is on the same page. Then the ambassador gets back on an airplane to return to the foreign embassy, where he or she will articulate with renewed precision what the nation's leaders are thinking.

For spiritual envoys such as us, the need is equally great for in-depth consultation from time to time. We cannot just assume that we already know what God is thinking. We have to ask—and then listen. Only then can we speak with confidence.

When I was a high school student growing up in an evangelical denomination, the youth group in every church across the country was named "Christ's Ambassadors," or more commonly, "C.A.'s." We were infused with the idea of representing Christ in a rapidly changing, often unraveling teen culture. There was a logo and even a theme song we sang at every meeting: "We are Christ's Ambassadors / And our colors we must unfurl . . ." and so on, until we reached the climax: "Proving duly that we're truly / Chri-i-i-st's Amm-baass-uh-dorrrrs!" It all sounds a bit goofy today (especially if you can recall the tune, a sprightly Sousa-style march).

But I cannot fault the concept. It accurately captured a necessary posture for Christian young people. It reminded us that we were on public display. It told us that our friends at school would draw their conclusions about Jesus from watching us.

None of that has changed today. People in the early twenty-first century are still perplexed about God. They sometimes think they'd like to forget about him altogether, but they keep being drawn back in his direction. What is he thinking? What does he want from you and me? If we lived the way he intended, would we be happy or miserable? What's the secret to a fulfilled and meaningful existence?

They need an approachable, informed, clearheaded, understandable ambassador.

3

The Christian "Brand"

All ambassadors worth their government paycheck know they are always on display. They are never just private individuals. The image and interests of the nation ride on those ambassadors' shoulders, twenty-four hours a day, seven days a week. They never get the luxury of speaking or acting just for themselves. They are always assumed to be speaking and acting on behalf of their homeland.

Their nationality is a brand. Like the mark of a hot branding iron on the flank of a West Texas steer, it is irreversible and unavoidable. This is not a bad thing; it is simply a fact. It goes wherever the bearer goes. Its significance is open for all to see.

As we all know, business corporations have adopted this language from the world of cattle raising and take their "brands" very seriously. They are forever analyzing and researching what will build a powerful brand in the super-competitive marketplace. They will spend millions to acquire product brands that they believe will strengthen their holdings.

Back in the 1980s, when New York publisher Random House was owned by the Newhouse media chain and was growing aggressively by acquisition, the following bit of anonymous humor made the rounds of the trade. At this point, Random House had already purchased Fawcett paperbacks, the prestigious Times Books line (from *The New York Times*), Fodor's travel guides, and Crown Publishing Group. The bogus news release read as follows:

RANDOM HOUSE ACQUIRES CATHOLIC CHURCH

New York—Random House has entered into an agreement with the Vatican to acquire the Catholic Church.

Founded by twelve poor Galileans in the Judea section of Israel during the early years of the first Millennium, the Church has grown into a multinational organization with more than 100 million members worldwide, an organization rivaled only by American Express/Shearson-Lehman in size. With its vast real estate holdings and its virtual monopoly in Afterlife Insurance, it has made itself a perennial presence on the list of Fortune 500 conglomerates.

The Church has also achieved great success as a publisher. It has launched the careers of many major authors, and its backlist includes works by Hans Kung, Thomas Aquinas, Matthew, Mark, Luke, and John.

"We feel this is a very good pairing," a spokesman for Random House stated earlier today when commenting on the acquisition. "Over its six decades of existence, Random House has published many important works: Joyce's *Ulysses*, as well as the works of Dr. Seuss and William Faulkner. We feel that the Bible—by general agreement, the greatest story ever told—is the perfect addition to the Random House catalog.

"We don't expect to tamper with the Church's management team," the spokesman continued. "How do you replace someone like the Pope? You don't. He's one of a kind. No, the Vatican has guided the Church through 20 centuries of uninterrupted growth, and you don't mess with an impressive record like that. The Church will thus operate as an independent division within Random House, and the Pope will report directly to Si Newhouse."

(Footnote to history: Random House itself was sold by the Newhouse family in 1998 to Bertelsmann AG, an even larger German conglomerate.)

We smile at the sophisticated humor. But imagine for a moment that the "brand" called *Christian* were for sale. Not just Roman Catholicism, but Protestantism and Orthodoxy as well: the whole package of all that bears the name of Christ. How much would you pay for this entity?

It holds many assets, to be sure—literary best sellers (as mentioned in the spoof), real estate, a highly motivated work force, a track record of helping people solve their deepest problems. It also contains a number of "downsides," to use another business term—various scandals, a serious lack of consistency, inter-group competition, to name just a few. All of these need to be weighed before you get out your checkbook.

To help you get a market sense, every August *Business Week* magazine and Interbrand, a global consulting firm, rank the leading brands in the world. In 2004, these were the most valuable names and their estimated worth:

1. "Coca-Cola" ($67 billion)
2. "Microsoft" ($61 billion)
3. "IBM" ($54 billion)

4. "GE" ($44 billion)
5. "Intel" ($33 billion)
6. "Disney" ($27 billion)
7. "McDonald's" ($25 billion)
8. "Nokia" ($24 billion)
9. "Toyota" ($23 billion)
10. "Marlboro" ($22 billion)[1]

The value of these brands is based upon their track records of consistency, quality, and service to the consumer. I once attended a seminar on creating powerful brands. The leader hammered the point that great brands have honed in on a promise to the customer—something the customer really wants. Having made the promise, the brand has then kept its word with unwavering tenacity. With Maytag, it is the dependability of its appliances. With FedEx, it is guaranteed overnight delivery—no slipups or excuses. With Southwest Airlines, it's being on time and low-cost.

"Building a brand is about creating and maintaining trust," said the seminar leader. "Once you promise that person something, never never never allow that trust to be compromised. You have to deliver every time. In this way you come to be a reliable brand, and people will reward you handsomely."[2]

I have visited McDonald's franchises in places as far-flung as Hong Kong, Sao Paulo, and Moscow. I can tell you that while the menu may have been posted in differing languages, the establishments all still looked and felt like McDonald's. The same upbeat service, the same standard of cleanliness, and the same taste of food prevailed regardless of which continent I was on. Every trip to the Golden Arches kept the "promise" of the brand.

Again I ask, if you were a wealthy entrepreneur, what would you be willing to pay for the rights to exploit the brand name "Christian"? Or would you decline the bidding altogether on the grounds that the label has accumulated too much liability over the centuries, and you'd rather start from scratch?

This is an exercise in absurdity, I admit. Jesus and his kingdom are clearly not for sale. I simply raise the question as a rhetorical device to get us thinking about the big picture of what Christianity has become in our world. If we are to be ambassadors, we need to be in touch with what people think when they hear or see our "label." It will help us communicate more effectively with them.

Robert Burns, the Scottish poet, wrote in 1786:

> Oh would some power the gifted give us
> To see ourselves as others see us!
> It would from many a blunder free us,
> And foolish notion.[3]

We all sincerely wish to avoid "many a blunder" in our lives as representatives of Jesus Christ. A great aid in that pursuit is to get out of our own skin and "see ourselves as others see us." Like it or not, most people on the planet do have an opinion about Christians, the same as they have an opinion about Microsoft or Toyota. Their experiences in the past, the hearsay in their circle of friends, their direct contact with actual Christians, the media reports they've read and seen—all of these have melded into a personal viewpoint. This opinion may be accurate or wildly distorted, fair or vindictive. But it is a very real perception, and as the old saying goes, "Perception is reality."

29

Attractive?

If it is true that there are smudges of dishonor on the Christian brand in today's world—and few would argue otherwise—part of the reason is that we don't have a clear delineation of who is allowed to wear the brand and who is not. Anyone can say, "Oh, yes, I'm a Christian," put a fish decal on their car, and then proceed to trash the values of the faith. Enforcing who belongs on the roster and who doesn't is nearly impossible, given the fractured nature of Christendom. The practice of excommunication has a sordid history all its own in centuries past, to the point that almost no one wants to return there.

But even among sincerely born-again, committed Christian people, we have frequent lapses of what business engineers would call "quality control." Daily lives don't always match up to the advertising. Divorce rates among churchgoers, for example, are not all that much better than among non-believers. For many Christians, intentions are good, but follow-through lags behind. And who is authorized to say, "Shape up, or else"? No one.

Compliance is unavoidably voluntary. We are all in the process of being "conformed to the likeness of [God's] Son, that he might be the firstborn among many brothers and sisters" (Rom. 8:29). If we all looked and thought and acted so like the One whose name we bear that observers said we seemed to be cut out of the same cloth, our brand would carry a lot more clout. This is indeed the goal.

In Titus 2, the apostle Paul gave a series of instructions to various groups in the church on the Mediterranean island of Crete. It is curious how often he included something on public impression. He asked the older men to be "worthy of respect" (v. 2). He asked older women to mentor younger women "so that no one will malign the word of God" (v. 5). He instructed Titus, as the pastor, to teach in such a way "that those who oppose you may be ashamed because they have nothing bad to say about us" (v. 8). He even advised slaves (who might have considered themselves at the bottom of the social order and thus powerless to cast any influence) that they should work diligently "so that in every way they will make the teaching about God our Savior attractive" (v. 10).

Would your neighbors and workplace acquaintances use that word to describe today's Christian community—*attractive*? If not, why not? What would it take to raise the cause of Christ to that level? These are questions worth pondering.

E. Stanley Jones once quoted an unnamed source who defined a Christian as "one who makes it easy for others to believe in God."[4] That is what Paul had in mind in his epistle. He wanted the average Cretan to say, "You know those Christians? I'm really intrigued with them. I'm going to check out what makes them so, so . . . what's the word? *Appealing*, perhaps."

Cretans, by the way, were not the most discerning lot; one of their own commentators, Epimenides, bluntly described them as "always liars, evil brutes, lazy gluttons" (Paul cites this in Titus 1:12). The apostle said to the believers in that society, "Let's rise above the rest! Let's stand out from the crowd for our positive qualities. Let's be shining candles in the moral haze." The life and walk of the Christian is intensely personal and even private in one sense. But there is no escaping the fact that others watch what we do and listen to what we say. None of us lives an entirely private life or practices a private faith. We each bear a portion of the responsibility for how Christians as a group are viewed.

In the late 1960s, when protesters took to the streets of America to decry the Vietnam War, they used a peculiar chant. The protesters knew that this was, in effect, the first war in human history to be covered by live television. Never before could people sit in their living rooms from Boston to Boise (and Bonn and Basel) and see what was going on at that moment. Thus the young people chanted to the nervous police with batons who sought to control them, "The whole world is watching! The whole world is watching!"

I mention those events not to make a statement about whether or not the protesters were justified in their actions. I simply say that they had the communication angle figured out correctly. They knew who their wider audience was. And they leveraged that knowledge to maximize their impact.

Four decades later, the world is more interconnected than ever. Information flies around the globe in seconds. Brand images are made—and ruined—across continents. Including the brand called "Christian."

We are stewards of that brand.

4

A Stone
for Stumbling

Before going much further in our quest for an attractive Christianity, we must stop and admit that certain things about our faith are unattractive. We can't pretend that everybody is going to love every part of the Christian message. Some parts, in fact, are downright hard to swallow.

That is why Isaiah prophesied that Israel's coming Messiah would be "a stone that causes people to stumble and a rock that makes them fall" (8:14)—a point reinforced by Paul in Romans 9:31–33. I must admit, this isn't my favorite epithet for the Son of God. I much prefer "Light of the World" and "Good Shepherd" and "Prince of Peace" and "Lamb of God." To say that we serve and honor "The Stumbling Stone" doesn't sound quite right.

But it is true nonetheless. We cannot pick and choose the parts of the gospel we find pleasant while shunting aside those we fear would alienate "the market." The insightful

British essayist Dorothy Sayers said it well in her famous essay "Creed or Chaos?":

> I believe it to be a grave mistake to present Christianity as something charming and popular with no offense in it. Seeing that Christ went about the world giving the most violent offense to all kinds of people, it would seem absurd to expect that the doctrine of his person can be so presented as to offend nobody. We cannot blink at the fact that gentle Jesus, meek and mild, was so stiff in his opinions and so inflammatory in his language that he was thrown out of the church, stoned, hunted from place to place, and finally gibbeted as a firebrand and a public danger. Whatever his peace was, it was not the peace of an amiable indifference; and he said in so many words that what he brought with him was fire and sword.[1]

What are the parts of the Christian message that make people squirm? Here is a list, starting with the one that gives rise to all the rest:

Some things are innately, objectively true—which means other things are not. This is the great stumbling stone for relativism. If there is a God who has revealed himself, and declared that certain things are good for humanity and others are harmful . . . lots of people these days would respond, "Well, I'm not so sure about that. It all depends on your point of view, you know? What is 'true' for you may not be 'true' for me, and vice versa. So let's just all relax and go out for coffee."

It was curious to note the resurrection of an old word in the wake of the September 11 horror: *evil*. Secular as well as religious commentators and politicians, no matter their previous leanings, could not settle for a softer, more nuanced adjective. This attack on innocent men and women on an ordinary Tuesday morning in the World Trade Center towers, they concurred, was undeniably *wrong*.

Once the dust and smoke cleared, however, and the funerals were over, ordinary life gradually resumed in America, and with it the suspicion about firm verities. Among the Christian teachings that continue to raise eyebrows today are the following:

None of us is entirely "good at heart." As such, that puts us at odds with a holy God. We would earnestly love to believe otherwise. Surely our mothers raised us to be decent folk. Politicians talk frequently about "the goodness of the American people." We're just pretty much all right, don't you think? A few bad apples show up each night on the news, of course, but they're the exception to the general rule.

The trouble with this line of thought is that we can hardly be objective about ourselves. We don't see our daily excursions into greed, fact-bending, sloth, and selfishness. Only an outside judge can determine our true character. As Paul admitted, "My conscience is clear, but that does not make me innocent. It is the Lord who judges me" (1 Cor. 4:4).

And unfortunately, God insists we have gotten off track from what he created us to be. He says, "All have turned away, all have become corrupt; there is no one who does good, not even one" (Ps. 14:3; see also Jesus's blunt words to the rich ruler in Luke 18:19).

We don't like to hear that.

Jesus has a solution for this disconnect with God—and it's the only solution. He came to earth to die for our redemption. He paid a gruesome price so we could be forgiven, if we're willing to ask. This was really quite extraordinary, this sacrifice for the human race. It has no equal and no alternate.

Television talk show interviewers love to press this last point with Christian guests. "Tell me," they intone with all seriousness, "is Jesus the only way to God?" They know that the real answer, the John 14:6 answer ("No one comes to the

Father except through me"), will be terribly out of vogue in contemporary culture.

But in fact, it has been problematic for a long time. More than seventy years ago, people used to speculate on whether the great Indian liberator Mahatma Gandhi was a Christian or not. After all, he had a picture of Jesus in his office, and none of Krishna or the Buddha. He loved to quote the Sermon on the Mount. The Christian hymn "Lead, Kindly Light" was his favorite prayer, he said.

Yet when queried about the exclusionary claims of the Son of God, he politely backed away. "An average Indian is as much a seeker after truth as the Christian missionaries are, possibly more so. . . . My position is that it does not matter what faith you practice, so long as the soul longs for truth." Gandhi, from the East, would get a rousing vote of agreement with that statement in Western societies today as well.

Jesus has a "change agenda" for each of us. He isn't content to let us keep being who we've always been up to now. He fully means to deal with our hypocrisy and aimlessness and lust and impatience and lack of compassion and all the rest. The point of our deciding to accept Christ is just the beginning; the subsequent follow-through will take the rest of our lives, turning us into much different people than we were at the start.

In fact, *part of his agenda is a call to self-sacrifice*, to give up my personal rights for the benefit of someone else. The New Testament says such radical, counterintuitive things as "Do nothing out of selfish ambition or vain conceit. Rather, in humility value others above yourselves, not looking to your own interests but each of you to the interests of the others" (Phil. 2:3–4). Isn't that downright un-American?!

More than a few times we will find ourselves stuttering, "But . . . but . . . I didn't really think I was signing up for this kind of overhaul." We have to decide afresh whether we're going to yield to the one we call "Master," or dig in our heels.

The Christian life is not a solitary endeavor; it's a group thing. Being a Christian entails being part of a motley collection called the church. This family is far, far from perfect. It frustrates us as often as it enthuses us. Like any family, it is heterogeneous; its members come in all ages, sizes, cultures, abilities, and sensitivities. Nobody gets their own way all the time. Everybody has to flex. And frequently, that isn't fun.

Evangelism is part of the package. The current culture tries to stigmatize this effort, of course, with words such as "proselytizing" or "forcing your religion down somebody else's throat." Anybody with a faith loyalty is expected to have at least the courtesy of keeping it to themselves. To do otherwise is considered bad manners.

And while some faiths are quite willing to play by these rules, authentic Christianity is not. Jesus's final words on earth, according to both Matthew 28 and Mark 16, were the Great Commission to "go and make disciples." We cannot scratch these lines from the sacred record, or deconstruct them into some alternate meaning. It is part of what the Savior asked us to do.

The fact not always admitted by critics of evangelism is that, in the modern marketplace of ideas and products, *everybody's pushing something.* We're all salespersons. We all engage in friendly propaganda for our sports team, our brand of car or truck, our definition of what the public schools should be, our strategy for beating the stock market. We're all trying to win "converts" to our point of view. Why should faith be any different?

The Bible is not just "a nice book." It's authoritative. Much as people might like to treat it simply as great literature from ages past, as one of the classics of human expression—it is more than that. It is the word not of mortals, but of God himself. Being such, it has the right to tell us what to do. We do not sit in judgment of it; it sits in judgment of us.

That makes the nonbeliever uncomfortable—*and the believer as well.* It impinges upon our autonomy. We all can point out passages we don't like. Ted Turner, the founder of CNN and an outspoken critic of Christianity, got a laugh once by saying, "If you're only going to have ten rules, I don't know if adultery should be one of them."[2] You and I would no doubt argue the opposite, that marital faithfulness is a great boon to human society. On the other hand, I confess I'm not wild about half a dozen other requirements of Scripture. Guess what—it doesn't matter. I'm not the master conductor of this concerto, and neither are you. Neither is Ted Turner. We all have to play by what's written on the page, or else we create dissonance.

All of these things are, in a sense, nonnegotiables. They're not up for debate. God has put them in place, whether we like them or not.

On the Other Hand . . .

However, we could make an even longer list of the good, desirable, attractive, enriching, elevating aspects of the gospel—the kinds of things everyone wants. Freedom from guilt. A personal God who truly loves you, understands you, and listens to you no matter what you've done or what you have to say. Fellow believers who care about your well-being. Peace in the soul. The possibility of supernatural answers to your problems—perhaps not always, but at least sometimes. Assurance of a future home in heaven. There's much to like about Christianity, even if "small is the gate and narrow the road that leads to life, and only a few find it" (Matt. 7:14).

All in all, the pros vastly outweigh the cons. The beautiful pearl, as Jesus described in his parable (Matt. 13:45–46), is definitely worth the price.

We ought not to camouflage the demands of the gospel in an effort to sell what Dietrich Bonhoeffer called "cheap grace." I'm always a bit leery of speakers who say things like "*just* come and give your heart to Jesus" or "*all* you have to do is . . ." as if it really were a very easy step to take, like buying a candy bar on sale. Excuse me, but salvation is a big deal. It's meant to change your entire life. Don't sell it short. If you do, the takers will find out the rest of the reality soon enough, and may feel misled.

Having said that, the fact remains that the benefits are infinitely more valuable than the perceived restrictions. Martyrs throughout the centuries have willingly gone to the burning stake or the firing squad rather than give up their place in the circle of God's love.

For those outside the circle who are troubled (or irritated) at the "nonnegotiables" we listed earlier, we must let them wrestle seriously and honestly. Meanwhile, here is a practical step for us: *don't make matters worse by thoughtless actions on our part.* The cross may indeed be offensive, but its ambassadors shouldn't be. If someone wishes to reject Jesus because he claimed to be the only way to God, so be it. But let them never reject Jesus because his truth was garbled or poorly demonstrated by a human spokesperson.

This is the point the apostle Peter was making when he wrote:

> If you are insulted because of the name of Christ, you are blessed, for the Spirit of glory and of God rests on you. If you suffer, it should not be as a murderer or thief or any other kind of criminal, or even as a meddler. However, if you suf-

fer as a Christian, do not be ashamed, but praise God that
you bear that name.

1 Peter 4:14–16

Of course we would all agree that criminal activity dishon-
ors our Lord, as Peter says. But notice that he also includes
the much milder misconduct of meddling as harmful to the
cause of Christ. He wants nothing to cloud the message of
the gospel. Let no human foible get in the way of the eternal
choices at stake.

This passage, by the way, is one of only three places in
which the Bible uses the term *Christian*. It was a name origi-
nally thought up by outsiders (see Acts 11:26). In the passage
above, Peter is very much thinking about the outside perspective. He is focused on what it means to be a "Christian"
in the wider culture. His whole book, in fact, is addressed
to "God's elect, exiles scattered throughout the provinces
of Pontus, Galatia, Cappadocia, Asia and Bithynia" (1 Peter
1:1), in other words, Gentile territory.

The Stumbling Stone is real. Some people will trip and
fall over it. They will wish God had made a different bargain
somehow, perhaps a merit-based scheme whereby good intentions would get them into heaven. But he didn't, and all
the human wishing in the world is not going to coax him
into changing his mind.

If people miss eternal life on this account, it will be a sad
outcome. Whatever the case, let us not make the leap of
faith any harder than it needs to be by our extraneous mis-
statements and off-putting behavior. "Make up your mind,"
Paul exhorted the Romans, "not to put any stumbling block
or obstacle in the way of a brother or sister" (14:13). How
much more so for the person who is only thinking about
whether to enter the family of God?

Part Two

Unintended Hindrances

5

What Fresh Eyes See

The grand hall of the United Nations complex in Ethiopia's capital city, Addis Ababa, had long been reserved. Invitations for the Saturday afternoon gala had been sent to hundreds of pastors, educators, church officials, and even politicians. The nicely designed programs were printed, folded, and ready in boxes. Dignitaries from the United States would soon be arriving at Bole International Airport. All the pieces were coming together for the great unveiling of International Bible Society's new, up-to-date translation in the Amharic language, a project some twenty years in the making.

All the pieces except one.

I had been in Addis Ababa working with my IBS colleagues for several days to prepare the way. Nearly everything was checked off our lengthy lists. The only remaining task: getting the actual shipment of Bibles cleared and released by the government customs bureau.

These Bibles—hardcover editions in navy blue and burgundy, a pocket-size New Testament with Psalms, even an impressive study Bible with extensive notes that was encased in both hardcover and bonded leather—had been printed outside Ethiopia due to technical limitations in the local printing industry. Starting out as two batches in Grand Rapids, Michigan, and Bungay, England, the two lots had been merged onto one ship, then sent down the west coast of Europe, through the Strait of Gibraltar, across the Mediterranean, through the Suez Canal, and finally into Djibouti, a dusty port on the Red Sea. Then a truck had loaded the two huge containers onto two trailers, one hooked behind the other tandem-style, and begun the rugged seven-hundred-mile trip inland over potholed roads up to the mile-and-a-half-high capital of Ethiopia. We had actually seen the big rig in the city with our own eyes, and rejoiced.

But first, the shipment would have to be "inspected" by a customs official. He would need to come to the containers, open them up, and prove to his satisfaction that they did actually contain what the bill of lading said, namely, Bibles (as opposed to, say, drugs or other contraband). The fact that the shipment already carried affidavits from the printers in the United States and in England—and furthermore, that independent agents had already "pre-inspected" and then sealed the containers on the original printing plant docks—made no difference. A bureaucrat in Addis Ababa would have to come take a look for himself.

(Confession time: I admit I am being cynical about another nation's rules and regulations, which is always a dangerous thing to do. I am sure that any Ethiopian, or other nationality, who has tried to get a travel visa from the American Embassy in their country could tell an equally exasperating tale of red tape. My point is not to scorn any nationality but rather to show how our eyes are opened to new insights whenever we enter unfamiliar terrain. We see things that others may miss.)

It was now Wednesday afternoon. "Solomon, what are we going to do?" I said to my Ethiopian colleague, who had already made a dozen phone calls requesting inspection. "We know our Bibles are sitting right out there on the edge of town, cooking in the hot sun. If we don't get our hands on them, Saturday's event is going to be a huge disappointment!"

He nodded in full agreement. He reviewed for me again the efforts he and his staff had made to break this logjam.

"Would it help at all," I asked, "if I went with you to the Customs Bureau to press the urgency of our need? Would the presence of a white American make them listen to you a little more? Or would that tend to have the opposite effect? Should someone like me stay out of sight?"

"No, I think it would be a help," Solomon replied. "They would see that an international organization is concerned about this."

So we drove downtown together. We arrived at a large complex at least a block square, where dozens of other trucks were lined up waiting for inspection, their drivers sitting in the shade killing time. We had been told that if our truck entered this maze of vehicles, the process would take up to two weeks. We were better off to have our driver stay outside the complex while we pleaded for an off-site review.

We walked into the crowded office building, moving from large room to large room until we found our place. Desks were jammed together in row upon row, paper stacks everywhere. Some desks had elderly computers, but in a city such as this with on-again, off-again electricity, their usefulness was limited. Employees glanced up briefly as we entered, then looked back down to the documents before them.

Naturally, I was of no help in communicating with these people, since I didn't speak Amharic. My only purpose was to lend a visual image to the scene. It took Solomon some thirty minutes to get a brief audience with the supervisor who held our fate in his hands. Meanwhile, I looked across the sea of paper, desks, and file cabinets. The white guy from America began indulging in a know-it-all flurry of analysis, mixed with a heavy dose of condescension.

I wanted to grab somebody by the collar and say, "Don't you realize you're obstructing progress and commerce in your country?! You want the economy to pick up, so people can escape the grip of poverty, right? So do we! We've fronted the money to bring in Bibles that will be sold in the marketplace, creating jobs for people who have none. And the product we bring is not frivolous; it's the Word of God. You have a Christian heritage in this country going back to the fourth century! You endorse what this Book says. For heaven's sake, just sign the paperwork so we can get on with this great benefit to your nation. Don't you understand that your delay is self-defeating? Why are you making things difficult for those who want to help you?"

Ah, yes, I had an eloquent speech in my head. It's a good thing I couldn't unleash it in their language. It would, of course, have only made matters much worse.

Meanwhile, the people before me that day went about their normal routine. They were simply concentrating on getting through their shift, moving enough paper to keep the boss happy, so they could collect a paycheck and feed their families for another week. The immediate was foremost, not the long-range.

Just then Solomon returned. "He says he will send out an inspection agent tomorrow," he reported. Both of us knew this was hardly a guarantee. Only time would tell. We had done as much as we could, however, and so we left to wait another night.

In the end, as often happens, the resolution took a different turn than we expected. The officials agreed that while we waited, we could go ahead and unload the Bibles by hand, a carton at a time, into a nearby church for safekeeping. At least then the truck driver could go on his way. We organized a brigade of young men with strong backs to do the unloading. Hours later, the inspector came to the church, opened a few cartons, and scratched his signature on the paperwork. We had our Bibles for the Saturday launch celebration just in the nick of time.

What Are *We* Missing?

I repeat, I tell this story not to denigrate the government employees of any nation. The same kind of story could be told in any setting, including the United States. For that matter, the same inefficiency prevails in a fair number of private corporations too. We've all had frustrating moments stuck in institutional molasses.

The people obstructing us are not necessarily bad people. They've just settled into ruts over the years. Some of them have even helped write thick procedure manuals to codify those ruts.

Certainly the church of Jesus Christ is as arthritic as the secular institutions we've been considering. We too have our traditions and protocols that must be honored, even if they work against our true goals. As an old wag put it, the seven last words of the church are these: "We never did it that way before."

We usually cannot see the forest for the familiar trees. Only when our setting is disrupted, when we travel someplace new, when we assume the role of a "foreigner," do we suddenly see the shortcomings and inefficiencies and contradictions. *Why in the world do they keep doing that?* we say to ourselves. *If they would just stop and think a minute. . . .*

Have you noticed what happens when you, for whatever reason, visit a different church for the first time? You may just be stopping by while on vacation. But all your senses are on heightened alert. You notice every detail: the crowded bulletin, the three-minute-late start to the service, the code language in the announcements that you can't understand, the bored expression on the face of the couple sitting next to you. You start to feel guilty after a while for all the critiques, but they keep popping up in front of you without your even trying.

Christians from other lands who come to America have insights that have never dawned on us "natives," and we would be wise to pay attention to them. Eugene Peterson wrote a few years ago:

> If you listen to a Solzhenitsyn or Bishop Tutu, or university students from Africa or South America, they don't see a Christian land. They see almost the reverse of a Christian land. They see a lot of greed and arrogance. And they see a Christian community that has almost none of the virtues of the biblical community, which has to do with a sacrificial life. . . . The attractive thing about America to outsiders is the materialism, not the spirituality. . . . What they want are cars and televisions. They're not [attracted to] our gospel.[1]

Now perhaps he overstates the case; you may know international believers who hold the American church in high esteem. But we must grant him at least half a point here. We are not in the best shape at living out the gospel, and we are myopic about it. Familiarity breeds passivity. We don't quite see what others with fresh eyes see.

The apostle Paul wrote to one of his best, healthiest churches (Philippi) this sobering sentence: "As I have often told you before and now tell you again even with tears, many live as enemies of the cross of Christ" (Phil. 3:18). Who would that be, we wonder? How wretched would a person have to be to qualify as an enemy of the cross? Who is public enemy number one as far as God is concerned?

When U.S., British, and other armed forces (the "coalition of the willing") invaded Iraq in 2003, soldiers were issued playing card decks with pictures of the fifty-six most wanted enemies. The ace of spades, of course, was Saddam Hussein. As soldiers handled the cards during their free time, they got familiar with the most important "bad guys" to be looking for.

Imagine who might be in the top fifty-six of heaven's enemies.

Osama bin Laden?

The church burners of Sri Lanka and other countries?

Michael Newdow, the California father who sued to get "under God" out of the U.S. Pledge of Allegiance?

The Massachusetts Supreme Court, which opened the door awhile back to gay "marriages"?

Well, before we get too busy writing our list, maybe we ought to see how Paul describes these enemies: "Their destiny is destruction . . . and their glory is in their shame" (v. 19). We could certainly nod agreement to those descriptors.

But those are only two of the four Paul gives in that verse. The others are: "Their god is their stomach"—in other words, they seem obsessed with food—and "their mind is set on earthly things." This last one is perhaps most damning of all. Their attention is pretty much wrapped up in the here and now. Matters of eternity are off at the edge somewhere; what really counts to these people are their homes, furnishings, cars, bank accounts, and all the other creature comforts of modern life.

That's all it takes to be named an enemy of Christ's cross?!

Yes, indeed, because the cross stands for sacrifice and self-denial. "Earthly things," on the other hand, are all about consumption and self-gratification.

Paul made his priorities clear in Colossians 3:1–2: "Since, then, you have been raised with Christ, set your hearts on things above, where Christ is seated at the right hand of God. Set your minds on things above, not on earthly things." In the following verses Paul gets very specific about what he means. He is calling for a sweeping change of values among those who bear the name of Christ.

To be fair, let it be said that nobody within the Christian family intends to be Christ's enemy. Nobody deliberately sets out to make him look bad. It just happens through lack of perception. We go to church, we do our various Christian activities the way we've always done them—and fail to notice the inconsistencies. We don't see what others see.

Big-picture thinking is absolutely crucial if we are to do our job as Christ's ambassadors. We can't bog down in individual concerns, traditions, or agendas. We have to look at the overall landscape and take note of what is causing what. Which actions are helping the cause, and which are unwittingly hindering it?

The next three chapters will spotlight ways we hinder God's kingdom without realizing it. The purpose is not to be vindictive. It is rather to lift our myopia and help us see what God himself sees.

Following that, we will spend twice as many chapters learning to do a better job.

6

Say What?

For starters, let's talk about how we talk. Words are not the only factor to consider in assessing our ambassadorship, but they are significant. We Christians speak a great deal, and "words are, of course, the most powerful drug used by mankind," as Rudyard Kipling taught us.

What matters is not the personal joy of sending words out of our mouth (or keyboard), but the impact they have on the other end. Original intent is one thing; received impact can be quite another. All too often, after a statement has landed crosswise on the hearer, we find ourselves backpedaling: "But what I *really* meant was . . ." There is simply no getting around the maxim, "Communication is not what I say; it's what you hear."

Hearing what other people hear is an acquired skill, to be sure. But it is not as hard as we might think. It simply means training your ear to put your words and sentences and paragraphs through the mental filter of the other person.

It means paying attention to how people naturally talk to each other, as well as to the media that shape us all. It even means checking back at times to see if what we say is getting through distortion-free.

When we apply "fresh ears" to Christian communication, we begin to notice at least four levels of problems.

Class 1: Words That Mystify

Some of what we say isn't bad; it just fails to connect with anything the hearer has encountered before. It belongs to a lexicon, a vocabulary that the person outside Christianity doesn't know.

Consider the Protestant church that advertises in the Yellow Pages the availability of "AWANA." Or the Catholic church that advertises "CCD." How is the average unchurched person to know that this signifies a club or class that seeks to anchor children in the teachings of the Christian faith? The names themselves are thick with mystery. ("AWANA," in case you didn't know, is an acronym for "A Workman And Not Ashamed," a phrase from 2 Timothy 2:15, one of the club's key memory verses. "CCD" stands for the multisyllabic "Confraternity of Christian Doctrine.")

Such groups can in fact be very well taught, providing an enriching experience for children. You'd just never know it from the public name.

In another church's ad in my city's phone book, the following hallmarks appear in a bold black box:

> **Fundamental**
> **Independent**
> **King James Only**
> **Separated**
> **Soul-Winning**

It would be interesting to take a poll of the neighbors around this congregation to see what they think each of those five terms signifies. The accuracy scores would probably be fairly low. But subliminally, the ad casts a certain mood of prickliness. This church sounds like the kind of place where one could easily say or do the "wrong" thing and get in trouble.

Another church advertises "Bus Ministry." Whatever does that mean? How do you minister to a bus?!

Yet another church a few pages away employs this slogan: "Declaring the Whole Counsel." That's good if you happen to be familiar with the apostle Paul's farewell address to the Ephesian elders in Acts 20 ("I did not shrink from declaring to you the whole counsel of God"—verse 27, RSV). If, however, you haven't read that particular verse (out of the Bible's 31,102 verses) in the last year or so, you're left scratching your head.

I do not mean to indict the practice of quoting Scripture. God's Word is indeed a sharp sword that can penetrate human defenses. But we have to choose our quotes wisely, with an ear for how contemporary hearers will respond.

How do you think the average motorist interprets the bumper sticker that says, "IN CASE OF RAPTURE, THIS CAR WILL BE UNMANNED"? The only definition of *rapture* most secular people know is ecstasy, as in perfume or chocolate or sex. Is the driver saying that if he sees an alluring female along the road, he'll jump out from behind the wheel to talk to her? If so, we have a major communication breakdown.

The most visible case of mystification in recent years was perhaps the large sign held up by a guy in a rainbow fright wig in numerous sports stadiums with the cryptic message "John 3:16." Tom Hennessy, columnist for the Knight-Ridder Newspapers, once explained in a witty article that this sign "does not refer to a player named John who bats third in the line-up and wears Number 16." He went on to bemoan the irritation of the "DM" (designated missionary) who blocked fans' views and distracted TV watchers. Nowhere in the Bible, he said, could he "find a passage which reads: 'Thou shalt go forth into thy nation's baseball parks and make a great nuisance of thyself in the name of the Lord.'"

Seriously, the more obtuse the Christian jargon, the tougher the communication challenge. The more we indulge in group-talk inside our churches, using our peculiar vocabularies built up over years of practice, the more odd we're going to sound as soon as we step outside. To represent the gospel effectively to today's culture, plain language is mandatory. The less "translation" needed the better.

John Wesley, one of the most brilliant men in eighteenth-century England, was Oxford-educated to the point he often wrote letters to his family in Latin. But his success in open-air preaching to the masses came because he learned the vocabulary of the common person.

> Calling an illiterate servant girl into his study, he said:
> "Now Mary, I want you to listen carefully to me. I am going to read one of my sermons to you, and each time I use a word or a phrase you do not fully understand, you are to stop me."
> So, with the help of Mary he learned a new language, and went forth in the power of the Holy Spirit to offer Christ freely to the people of England in a tongue they spoke and understood.[1]

The result was the great Methodist awakening.

Class 2: Words That Overwhelm

Sometimes our words are not obscure, but instead they carry a tone of triumphalism—we Christians are going to win this or that cultural battle, and don't you forget it. Some Christian radio programs are infamous for urging listeners to "take back America" from the godless hordes that are said to have overrun it. The language of war, of showdown, of confrontation are employed to motivate response.

In a nation that one religious leader, the Dalai Lama, correctly dubbed a "spiritual supermarket,"[2] those are inflammatory words. They raise the hackles of all who view things differently, stirring up fears of coercion.

Just exactly how "Christian" this country has been throughout its history is a topic I addressed at length in my earlier book *Sinners in the Hands of an Angry Church*. Without returning to that debate, I will focus instead on the current scene. If our declared goal is to make friends for the cause of Christ today, we need to consider a different approach, one that lowers apprehensions and increases winsomeness.

In responding to the dreadful tsunami that struck South Asia at the end of 2004, one denomination's relief coordinator in Thailand told a reporter that his church had been "praying for a way to make inroads" with a particular ethnic group. Again, the imagery of battle, of penetrating a stubborn pocket of resistance, did not win him favorable press. His enthusiasm was overly joyful when he called the tsunami "a phenomenal opportunity."[3] Those devastated Thai Buddhists whose livelihoods and even children had been washed away by the monster wave could hardly share his cheerfulness. We fellow believers know what he meant and do not question his sincerity. But we wish he had chosen more sensitive language.

The trouble is that, too often, we forget who all is listening. We think we're having a private conversation with people of like mind, when in fact the whole world is tuned in. This is particularly the hazard of Christian broadcast media. Next time you're in your car listening to a Christian call-in show, look out the window at the drivers in the next lane, and think about the fact that at that moment they could be listening to the same station as you. Does that make you feel good, or nervous?

There is certainly a place for private dialogue. Certain topics are "family only." There's a good reason, for example, why your local church does not hold its periodic business meetings in the city park, with everyone from skateboarders to stroller-pushing moms listening in. Debates over strategic initiatives and spending decisions should rightly be held among members behind closed doors.

But even then, those outside the building should be referred to respectfully and realistically. They too are persons made in the image of God, who gave them the right of personal choice. If they wish to embrace the Good News of salvation, that will be wonderful. They ought not, however, to be poleaxed into submission.

Class 3: Words That Antagonize

Closely related to confrontation talk is a third category: words that seek to rile the individual who reads them. Some Christians seem to have gotten the notion that God's cause is advanced by in-your-face hostility and bad manners. Why else would they make and sell a T-shirt with a sketch of a fallen giant that reads:

Fine
Don't Keep God's Commandments
Just Don't Come Crying To Me
When You End Up
Flat On Your Face Like
GOLIATH

Another one displays an eerie white shape bearing the black numerals "666," surrounded by these words:

Tattoo Your Soul
Burn In Hell

Even though large percentages of the general public tell pollsters they don't believe in a literal place of eternal punishment, the bumper stickers keep coming:

READ THE BIBLE—IT'LL SCARE THE HELL OUT OF YOU

GOT JESUS? IT'S HELL WITHOUT HIM

JESUS IS COMING, AND BOY IS HE MAD!

This kind of aggression is great for making enemies. Yes, I am sure that if we looked hard enough, we could find one or two converts who were impacted by such a harsh message and got right with God as a result. But does that justify the thousands upon thousands who were nauseated by such tasteless scaremongering?

Some will point out that Jesus, and Old Testament prophets as well, used fairly pungent language on occasion. Yes, they did—but to whom? Religious hypocrites who claimed God's "brand" but lived quite the opposite: Pharisees, scribes, corrupt priests of the temple, and the like.

On the contrary, we don't see our Lord insulting Roman legionnaires, although many of them no doubt led promiscuous lives. In contrast, he reached out to centurions and tax collectors and immoral women when he didn't even have to. This Savior built bridges, not walls.

58

The push for acceptance of homosexuals is a reality in today's American culture, and many activists want the Word of God to bend further than it will. This is one of those "stumbling stones" we considered in chapter 4. But is the dialogue really helped by sarcastic signs that say, "GOD CREATED ADAM & EVE, NOT ADAM & STEVE"? Does this shed helpful light on what the Bible actually says about homosexual practice, and why it says what it does? Would those involved in this lifestyle be more likely to consider the biblical way as a result? I think not.

That same Word of God is clear when it advises us, "Be wise in the way you act toward outsiders; make the most of every opportunity. Let your conversation be always full of grace, seasoned with salt, so that you may know how to answer everyone" (Col. 4:5–6).

Class 4: Words That Manipulate

The most grievous abuse of language is perhaps when Christian rhetoric is used to manipulate believers into doing something the speaker wants—usually, to part with their money. This happens from time to time inside some church services, forgetting that the occasional visitor can take notice. But much more widely and obviously, of course, it happens on Christian broadcasts, especially television. (Television is a far more expensive medium than radio, and thus the programmers are under greater pressure to raise funds.)

When viewers are cajoled into donating in order to "receive a triple blessing from God this very month!" non-Christians roll their eyes in disgust. The spiritual discipline of *giving* has been morphed into *bargaining*. If I send in a certain amount to the televangelist, God will give me a refund, with extra.

The motivation is not to advance God's kingdom nearly so much as it is to cash in personally.

I say this not to deny the truth of Luke 6:38, the favorite text of the prosperity preachers. Jesus did indeed say, "Give, and it will be given to you. A good measure, pressed down, shaken together and running over, will be poured into your lap." But allow me to follow up with an odd question: *Give to whom?* What was Jesus talking about on this occasion?

The previous two paragraphs are about loving *your enemies* and doing good to *those who hate you.* "If someone takes your coat, do not withhold your shirt. Give to everyone who asks you" (vv. 29–30). "If you lend to those from whom you expect repayment, what credit is that to you? Even sinners lend to sinners, expecting to be repaid in full. But . . . lend to them without expecting to get anything back. Then your reward will be great" (vv. 34–35).

This is the run-up to the oft-quoted "Give, and it will be given to you. . . ." Jesus is talking about being gracious and generous with unbelieving, even unscrupulous neighbors who have no fear of God. In such cases, he says, God will make sure that your needs are taken care of regardless.

I have a hard time seeing how today's aggressive fund-raisers on television qualify for the proceeds of this text. Especially when some of them have already been so effective. The world's largest Christian TV network was recently reported to have stashed away cash, short-term investments, and long-term investments of about two hundred and eighty million dollars—more than the entire annual operating budget of all but a handful of ministries. Its husband-and-wife founders take a combined salary of more than eight hundred thousand dollars a year. *Dateline NBC* documented that one of America's foremost healing evangelists stays in two-thousand-dollar-a-night hotel rooms when he travels to his various events and lives in a 3.5-million-dollar house with eight bedrooms and nine bathrooms in a Southern California gated community. Across the country in less expensive middle America, another female television teacher was found by the *St. Louis Post-Dispatch* to be living in a two-million-dollar home and enjoying the use of a ten-million-dollar private jet.

Yet all three fervently look into the cameras and urge viewers to send still more donations in order to receive God's best in their lives.

To its credit, *Charisma* magazine, which tracks these kinds of ministries, ran a no-holds-barred critique in its July 2004 issue entitled "Crazy Money." Said Larry Tomczak, longtime charismatic leader, author, and now pastor near Atlanta, "I wish this craziness were the exception, but it seems it is becoming the rule. . . . If we don't bring some correction to their behavior soon the testimony of the American church will be ruined. . . . We are turning people off, especially the younger 'make it real' generation, when we manipulate people to fill offering plates."[4]

The use of words may bring short-range gains, but the long-range damage to our credibility is enormous. Too many of our cynical neighbors have already shut down, concluding that when it comes to the church, "It's all about money, isn't it?" Jesus and his disciples never profiteered from their ministries, and neither should we. Whatever we say about giving must ring one hundred percent authentic.

If any Christian needs permission to ignore high-pressure fund appeals, they need look no further than 2 Corinthians 9:7, which says giving should be done "not reluctantly or under compulsion." God isn't interested in that kind of money.

The Ministry of Welcome

The larger point here is that our words are windows into the soul and heart of who we truly are. If we want others to join us in this walk of faith, coming to love and serve the Christ we know, they will want to do so only if they see an admirable model. Our words reveal, intentionally and unintentionally, our inner character. Sometimes we do not even know what we have "telegraphed" by the way we speak and write.

Rich Nathan, senior pastor of Vineyard Church of Columbus, Ohio, writes in his book *Who Is My Enemy? Welcoming People the Church Rejects,* "We must stop shutting the door of the kingdom in the faces of those whom God is inviting in. We will reserve our harshest judgments for ourselves. As we carry out our ministry of welcome, we will season our moral stances with profound mercy and compassion for a hurting world."[5]

A couple of bumper stickers are currently sold that might actually be useful. One empathizes with how our current situation must look from above, and says:

DON'T BLAME GOD FOR THE THINGS PEOPLE DO

The other is a good restraint on Christians who tend to forget they are constantly watched by others. It simply reads:

HOW WOULD JESUS DRIVE?

7

One Lord, One Faith, 31 Flavors

Suppose you were unchurched, but you came to a crossroads in your life where for the first time you actually wanted to explore spirituality. Simply making money all week and chasing parties on the weekend were no longer fulfilling your inner soul. The "God-shaped vacuum" that Blaise Pascal wrote about in the 1600s was making itself felt. You decided to give an honest look at Christianity.

If so . . . where would you start?

The first complication you would face would be "which kind of Christianity?" There's a church just down the street—but what about the other one a block farther? Are they the same? No, the names don't match at all. So which one is authentic? How would a novice figure out whom to trust?

Christendom has become an incredibly fractured entity. The *Yearbook of American and Canadian Churches* (2004 edition) indexes 216 different U.S. denominations, from *A* (Advent Christian Church) almost to *Z* (the last entry is Wisconsin Evangelical Lutheran Synod). Along the way you'll find such unique varieties as the Cumberland Presbyterian Church, the Old German Baptist Brethren, the General Church of the New Jerusalem, and—take a deep breath for this one—House of God, Which Is the Church of the Living God, the Pillar and Ground of the Truth, Inc. It's more overwhelming than a trip to Baskin-Robbins.

The inquirer understandably wonders, "Do these all follow the same God?" (Answer: Yes.) "Are they all based on the same Bible?" (Answer: Yes.) "So are they all pretty much the same?" (Answer: No!)

Some of the distinctions are serious theological matters, where sincere and devoted people reading the same Bible have come to different conclusions. These differences should not be brushed aside as frivolous or arcane. Perhaps one group is partially mistaken, but we don't know for sure, do we? Perhaps they have it exactly right, and will be vindicated in heaven. Or perhaps the precise truth is partway between the positions of two differing groups, and we just haven't realized it yet. We all have some homework left to do.

Other distinctions, however, are not very theological at all. They are more cultural in nature. Some are mere accidents of history. Two or three groups believe essentially the same thing, but they got started in different decades (or even centuries) in different parts of the country, and so they continue. All this is in some ways an unintended by-product of *Protest*antism. Our sixteenth-century forebears felt the need to *protest* against the corruption of the medieval

Catholic Church by forming an alternative. The spinoffs have never stopped.

Alexis de Tocqueville, the young French magistrate who toured America in 1831 to study the new democracy, said he was quite amazed to see how prodigiously the people of the New World formed new groupings:

> Americans of all ages, all conditions, and all dispositions constantly form associations . . . of a thousand . . . kinds, religious, moral, serious, futile, general or restricted, enormous or diminutive. The Americans make associations to give entertainments, to found seminaries, to build inns, to construct churches, to diffuse books, to send missionaries to the antipodes [opposite sides of the globe]. . . . If it is proposed to inculcate some truth or to foster some feeling by the encouragement of a great example, they form a society. Whenever at the head of some new undertaking you see the government in France, or a man of rank in England, in the United States you will be sure to find an association. . . .
>
> The English often form great things singly, whereas the Americans form associations for the smallest undertakings.[1]

So it's in our blood, apparently. We just naturally tend to set up organizations and denominations and fellowships and coalitions. Why do we do this so readily? Tocqueville had an explanation worth considering.

In aristocracies (such as his own country), he said, kings and nobles with lots of power could make things happen pretty much on their own. They had the money, the connections, and the employees to cut a wide swath single-handedly. But in America, the Frenchman noted, "all the citizens are independent and feeble; they can do hardly anything by themselves, and none of them can oblige his fellow men to lend him their assistance."[2] They have no choice but to form an association. And once they do, there is no potentate around to tell them to stop it.

The standard Protestant response to all this is to say that you can't turn back the clock of history. What's done is done. A few well-meaning mergers of denominations have been tried in the past, with mixed results. The ten-million-member Methodist Church, for example, added almost a million Evangelical United Brethren back in 1968 to form the United Methodist Church—but today the combined total comes to just around 8.2 million.

A more recent response has been to question the denominational paradigm altogether. "Community churches" are springing up everywhere, and often seem to grow the fastest. Such congregations position themselves almost entirely in local terms. They are either truly independent and self-governing, or else they carefully hide whatever affiliation they may have. The need to cooperate with other churches or organizations on larger projects, such as missionary efforts, is kept in the shadows. Our era is indeed becoming more post-denominational.

This is a counterintuitive trend, by the way, compared to the commercial world. When it comes to cars or restaurants or clothing or groceries, national brand means everything. "Mom-and-Pop" enterprises struggle to get attention against the big names. Who wants to eat at Smith's Restaurant when there's an Olive Garden or an Outback Steakhouse nearby, with familiar quality and atmosphere? In the world of churches, however, a denominational label has almost become a liability.

Moreover, few seekers bring a "brand preference" to their search (with the possible exception of those from a Catholic heritage). They just want to find the reality of knowing Christ, and wonder why his various people can't get along better. Why, when they scan the church ads in the Saturday newspaper, do they see competitive slogans such as "Friendliest Church in Town"? Why, for that matter, do so many church names start with the word "First," as if to claim seniority over other congregations?

No wonder perplexity abounds. No wonder those with a yearning for spiritual wholeness get sidetracked and confused. "A fragmented church is not much help to a fragmented world," says historical theologian Justo L. González.[3]

What can we do, given our various heritages, to minimize this problem? Realistically speaking, we are never going to be able to unify and standardize ourselves across the nation the way Texaco or Shell does, so that anybody entering any service center (read: local church) in any town gets the same quality products, the same attentive service, in the same pleasant atmosphere. We Christians are always going to be a "mixed bag." Uniform franchising is never going to happen.

But having admitted that, let us go on to note some things we *can* do to reduce the confusion. While allowing for local and denominational distinctives, here are three steps we can take that will make a big difference in reaching our common goal, which is to uphold the cause of Christ to a curious (if partly skeptical) world.

Major in the Majors

We need to adopt the attitude of the apostle Paul in Corinth—a society prone to partisan loyalties—who wrote, "I resolved to know nothing while I was with you except Jesus Christ and him crucified" (1 Cor. 2:2). Christ is the central answer for human need. To lift him up is the most important thing we can do. People are not looking today for a creed so much as a Savior.

This is not to say that doctrinal distinctives are unimportant. They do matter and ought not to be swept aside. Whoever takes the Scripture seriously will come to definite conclusions about its significance on a variety of topics. And some of these can justifiably be classified as "major."

The most important doctrine for us all, however, is that of redemption. Helping men and women cross the line from darkness to light needs to take priority over all other debates. Not just once a year during a special campaign. All the time, month in, month out.

Part of our problem is a subconscious one, in that we carry a lifelong craving for novelty. We get too easily bored with "the old, old story of Jesus and his love," as the song puts it. We're more intrigued by that which is unique and new and complicated. We think pastors who keep repeating the offer of forgiveness of sins aren't very creative. Can't they come up with something we haven't already heard a hundred times?

Paul taunted the Corinthians, after they had split up into at least four factions, about being too sophisticated for their own good.

> Already you have all you want! Already you have become rich! You have begun to reign—and that without us! . . . We are fools for Christ, but you are so wise in Christ! We are weak, but you are strong! You are honored, we are dishonored! . . .
>
> I am writing this not to shame you but to warn you as my dear children. . . . Some of you have become arrogant.
>
> 1 Corinthians 4:8, 10, 14, 18

What may be simple and overworked to those of us who have grown up in church may be exactly the Good News an outside person is seeking. The more we stay in touch with their needs and issues, the more we will focus on the core of the gospel. That is what the world needs more than anything else.

Rediscover the "City-Church" Concept

Most of us have stopped noticing that the book of Acts and the Epistles never mention more than one church per city. Antioch, Ephesus, Philippi, Rome, Thessalonica—so far as we can tell, the believers in each of these places were unified as a family. (Paul's letter to "the churches in Galatia" is not an exception to this rule; Galatia was a province, not a single city.)

Granted, the people did not seem to meet under one roof—they could hardly have afforded to construct such an edifice in those early days. They gathered in private homes all across the city. But they were a "body" nonetheless, under unified leadership, caring for one another and supporting each other's walk of faith. They belonged to each other.

Some contemporary pastors are working to reclaim this identity. On a citywide basis they are meeting for prayer and mutual encouragement. They are speaking among themselves and to their congregations about the idea of "the Church at Denver" or "the Church at Indianapolis," by which they mean all of God's people in that locale, regardless of which specific theology they embrace or which building they use.

I have a feeling that some of our greatest luminaries in church history would heartily agree with this. Martin Luther said once:

> I ask that men make no reference to my name, and call themselves not Lutherans, but Christians. What is Luther? My doctrine, I am sure, is not mine, nor have I been cru-

cified for anyone. St. Paul, in 1 Corinthians 3, would not allow Christians to call themselves Pauline or Petrine, but Christian. How then should I, poor, foul carcass that I am, come to have men give to the children of Christ a name derived from my worthless name? No, no, my dear friends; let us abolish all party names, and call ourselves Christians after him whose doctrine we have.

Two hundred years later, John Wesley said much the same:

I should rejoice (so little ambitious am I to be at the head of any sect or party) if the very name [Methodist] might never be mentioned more, but be buried in eternal oblivion.[4]

And a hundred years after that, Charles Haddon Spurgeon, perhaps the greatest Baptist preacher who ever lived, said:

I say of the Baptist name, let it perish, but let Christ's name last for ever. I look forward with pleasure to the day when there will not be a Baptist living.[5]

Well, none of these three great men's wishes have yet come true. We could, however, turn a stronger spotlight on this concept. We could do more local demonstrations of working together across denominational lines for common causes, whether in evangelism, ministry to the poor, guidance to troubled youth, or other needs. If we did, the watching world would see more of what unites us and less of what divides us.

Take Conflict Seriously

When tensions arise and differences divide the witness of the Christian community, it is all too tempting to sit back and say one of two things:

- In cases where we are only an outside observer of the conflict: "Well, it isn't my issue. If I got involved, it would only make matters worse. They'll work it out eventually."
- In cases where we are a participant on one side or the other: "But this is worth going to the mat. Truth must be defended, or it will be lost."

Maybe so. But let us never forget the price it costs us all. Let us always keep the "outside view" in mind. Let us stop and ask ourselves: "Could I adequately explain this struggle to a nonbeliever? Would he or she see the logic of this skirmish?"

Karen Mains tells a poignant fable in her book *The Key to a Loving Heart*, entitled "A Wedding Like No Other":

The wedding guests have gathered in great anticipation; the ceremony to be performed today has been long awaited. The orchestra begins to play an anthem and the choir rises in proper precision. The bridegroom and his attendants gather in front of the chancel. One little saint, her flowered hat bobbing, leans over to her companion and whispers, "Isn't he handsome?" The response is agreement, "My, yes. The handsomest."

One by one, the bridesmaids, heralds of the nuptials, begin to stride in measured patterns. Several flower girls sow rose petals upon the white, unmarked aisle cloth. The sound of the organ rises, a joyous announcement that the bride is coming. Everyone stands and strains to get a proper glimpse of the beauty—then a horrible gasp explodes from the congregation. This is a bride like no other.

In she stumbles—something terrible has happened! One leg is twisted; she limps pronouncedly. The wedding garment is tattered and muddy; great rents in the dress leave her scarcely modest. Black bruises can be seen welting her bare

71

arms; the bride's nose is bloody. An eye is swollen, yellow and purple in its discoloration. Patches of her hair look as if they had actually been pulled from her scalp.

Fumbling over the keys, the organist begins again after his shocked pause. The attendants cast their eyes down. The congregation mourns in speechless silence. Surely the Bridegroom deserved better than this! That handsome Prince who has kept himself faithful to his love should find consummation with the most beautiful of women—not this. His bride, the church, has been fighting again.[6]

The ancient book of Judges tells two stories of what can happen when groups of differing heritage within the same nation get upset with each other. The conflicts are similar, but the outcomes are radically opposite. As such, they form a valuable lesson for us in our modern situation.

The first is in the beginning of chapter 8, just as Gideon's little band has finished devastating the powerful Midianites, to the astonishment of all. Gideon, as you will recall, was one of the Bible's most tentative, self-doubting leaders. He never thought he could accomplish much of anything. His clan was "the weakest in Manasseh," he told the angel at first, "and I am the least in my family" (6:15).

The battle tide begins to go his way, however. He jubilantly calls for reinforcements from other tribes—Naphtali, Asher, and Ephraim. A great victory is won for God's people.

When the dust settles, the strong tribe of Ephraim is chagrined that they played so minor a role so late in the stunning ambush that succeeded.

> Now the Ephraimites asked Gideon, "Why have you treated us like this? Why didn't you call us when you went to fight Midian?" And they challenged him vigorously.
>
> 8:1

Gideon, in their minds, has grown a little too big for his britches. He needs to be reminded that Ephraim has always been a premier tribe. To call for their help only as an afterthought was a serious faux pas.

This situation could erupt in a feud. After all, feelings have been hurt. Reputations have been tarnished. Trouble is brewing.

Gideon, however, is a man of peaceful intent. He doesn't need to brag about his accomplishments. He chooses, instead, the route of self-deprecation.

> But he answered them, "What have I accomplished compared to you? Aren't the gleanings of Ephraim's grapes better than the full grape harvest of Abiezer [his own clan]? God gave Oreb and Zeeb, the Midianite leaders, into your hands. What was I able to do compared to you?" At this, their resentment against him subsided.
>
> 8:2–3

Gideon's calm spirit defuses the smoking wick of tribalism. That word, I know, may remind the reader of such faraway places as Rwanda or Kosovo. But tribalism is a menace in our Western religious world too. It can flare up at a moment's notice, to the embarrassment of all. We would all do well to ask ourselves these questions:

- Do I feel in competition with other "tribes," i.e., churches, denominations, or parachurch ministries?
- Do I truly *listen* to the other side, or simply await my next turn to speak?
- Do I take the other side seriously, or am I just waiting for them to "see the light"?

- How quickly do I start defending myself and my "tribe"?
- Do I have something of "the Ephraim attitude"?
- Have I learned the truth of Proverbs 15:1—"A gentle answer turns away wrath, but a harsh word stirs up anger"?

D. L. Moody is often credited with the wise saying "The world has yet to see what God can do through a person who doesn't care who gets the credit." Gideon did not mind who got the credit for defeating the oppressors. He only cared that God's people were safe once again.

The second story of conflict from Judges occurs in chapters 11–12. Once again Israel has fallen into sin, triggering the judgment of God in the form of an Ammonite occupation. And once again, an unlikely leader emerges. His name is Jephthah—son of a prominent father but a prostitute mother. For that reason, he was evicted from home at an early age and has become a renegade troublemaker. You might even call him the leader of a terrorist cell. After all, he was forced to fight for everything he had gotten in life, until that became his personality.

Believe it or not, God uses him. The Lord channels Jephthah's energy into a useful cause. (Apparently, God has ways of using both the timid and the turbulent.)

And once the battle is won . . . here come the pesky Ephraimites again!

The Ephraimite forces were called out, and they crossed over to Zaphon and said to Jephthah, "Why did you go to fight the Ammonites without calling us to go with you? We're going to burn down your house over your head."

12:1

Some things never change, it seems.

Jephthah is not about to sit still for this kind of trash talk. His adrenalin surges, and fire begins to blaze in his eyes. His voice gets louder and louder as he spits out the words:

> I and my people were engaged in a great struggle with the Ammonites, and although I called, you didn't save me out of their hands. When I saw that you wouldn't help, I took my life in my hands and crossed over to fight the Ammonites, and the Lord gave me the victory over them. Now why have you come up today to fight me?
>
> 12:2–3

The text reports that he immediately re-musters his troops for a showdown with the Ephraimites. The army of Gilead chokes off the crossing point of the Jordan River and proceeds to slaughter every Ephraimite trying to get home again. They identify who's who by a clever test of pronunciation: "Say 'shibboleth,'" which means "floods" (12:6). The men of Ephraim mumble "sibboleth" instead, due to their accent. Swords flash instantly.

When the blood finally stops flowing, a dreadful loss of life has occurred. "Forty-two thousand Ephraimites were killed at that time," reports Judges 12:6. Think of the horror . . . forty-two thousand funerals . . . forty-two thousand graves on the hillsides. By comparison, this is not far from the total loss of American life during the entire Vietnam War (some fifty-eight thousand).

This account teaches us that when tribal instincts take over, a great many people can get hurt. Defending the honor of one's group sounds so needful in the beginning, but the toll can be devastating. In our contemporary situation, how many people never get to experience *eternal* life because of infighting among Christians? How many spiritual casualties result from unnecessary conflict within the family of God?

This is clearly not what a loving heavenly Father intends.

If Alexis de Tocqueville was right in saying that the American proclivity for associations has something to do with the absence of power brokers in our society, perhaps we ought to stop and remember that Christians *do* have a Supreme Authority after all, the King of kings and Lord of lords. One has to wonder how many times over the past five hundred years (or more) Jesus Christ has looked down from heaven and said, "Please don't do that. We really don't need yet another duplication of effort. We certainly don't need internecine attacks and insinuations. You're confusing the very people I'm most concerned about. Never mind your self-preservation; focus instead on the mission for which I came to earth in the first place: 'to seek and to save what was lost'" (Luke 19:10).

The goal of representing Christ effectively in a dark world must never be hindered by the personal and group agendas of his people.

8

Consistency, Please

We have examined two potential hindrances to the gospel: our words, and our splintered positioning. One more topic remains on our list, and it is perhaps more significant than the other two combined. It is the way Christians actually live day-to-day.

Jesus was the one who spelled out a fairly demanding standard when he said, "Every good tree bears good fruit, but a bad tree bears bad fruit. A good tree cannot bear bad fruit, and a bad tree cannot bear good fruit. . . . Thus, by their fruit you will recognize them" (Matt. 7:17–18, 20). He was constantly pointing out the gap between profession and reality. He didn't mind confronting religious aristocrats of his day with such words as "You hypocrites! You are like whitewashed tombs, which look beautiful on the outside but on the inside are full of the bones of the dead" (Matt. 23:27).

Some modern critics speak almost that harshly about organized religion. When they do, whether on the op-ed page of the newspaper, in TV commentaries, or in Internet chat rooms, we grumble that they're biased and mean-spirited—which is often true. But we also know deep in our hearts that our walk and talk need to be better synchronized. When deeds fall short of precepts, criticism is bound to come, and we cannot complain about it. We have in recent years endured more than a few such episodes.

Spectacular Embarrassments

Any American Christian who was around in 1987 can still remember the dismay and chagrin we felt when the PTL empire collapsed in disgrace. We hoped our neighbors and co-workers wouldn't generalize about us too. Then in February 1988, a major critic of Jim and Tammy Faye Bakker, televangelist Jimmy Swaggart, crashed just as spectacularly in his own moral scandal. We groaned again.

It couldn't get any worse, we assumed. Surely every Christian leader would keep his life clean from that point onward. The name of Christ would surely suffer no further sabotage.

But here we are more than fifteen years later . . . and the bad news continues. To cite just two recent examples:

- An eloquent spokesperson for moral living, an adviser to U.S. presidents, a compiler of a best-selling book of virtue stories from the ages that thousands of parents have used to shape their children's character . . . was found to have a serious gambling problem. His losses tallied up to more than eight million dollars. An editor of *Washington Monthly* magazine (which exposed the story) wrote, "By furtively indulging in a costly vice that destroys millions of lives and families across the nation, [he] has profoundly undermined the credibility of his word on this moral issue."[1]

- We learned not long ago that a current impresario on Christian television shelled out four hundred and twenty-five thousand dollars to a former employee in 1998 to shush up allegations of a homosexual encounter with him. The money wasn't enough; the young man ended up raising the ante to ten million dollars, and soon it all hit the front page of the *Los Angeles Times*. The accusation has not been proven as of the writing of this book—but why would a prominent minister pay that much money if it were untrue? Why wouldn't he have seized the initiative and said to his constituency long ago, "Somebody is falsely accusing me of immorality, and I wanted you to hear it from me first. He wants money to keep quiet—but he's not getting a dime of your donation funds. This is pure blackmail." The fact that nothing was said in advance stokes the suspicion that the young man's story has some basis. If not, then the televangelist's *spending* decisions are highly questionable.

Again, we cringe. *Why do we keep shooting ourselves in the foot?* we ask. How in the world are people supposed to believe that Christ offers a better way of life when his most visible advocates keep contradicting his message?

What about Us?

But then, before we get too carried away with reproaching the eloquent and famous . . . we probably ought to stop and ask how we ourselves, in our own small arenas of life, are doing. What does the average secular person see in our lives that reinforces the message of the gospel, not undermines it?

They see us going to church. They hopefully see us showing up for work on time, and putting in a full day's effort once we get there. They see us taking adequate care of our children. They may even see us volunteering at the local school or hospital. All of these are notable.

But in other areas, they may have cause to question.

Take, as one example, our *choice of media*. Nearly every Christian I know is disturbed by the spreading sleaze, foul language, and gratuitous violence on television and in the movies. Eloquent protests and even boycotts have been raised to try to get Hollywood to quit dragging viewers through the moral gutter.

The only trouble is, Christians don't seem quite disturbed enough to stop watching that media. After the Super Bowl 2004 debacle with entertainer Janet Jackson's infamous "wardrobe malfunction," TV producers were roundly criticized for their cavalier attitude; even the Federal Communications Commission (FCC) summoned some of them to explain. The producers scored a major counterblow, however, when they noted that many of TV's raciest programs were getting ratings in markets with high church attendance (Atlanta, Dallas, Salt Lake City, among others) that were just as strong as their ratings in "ungodly" places like New York or San Francisco.

We have to admit that old-fashioned "legalism" in the Christian community is no longer much of a problem. Older folk still sometimes try to tell horror stories about how, as children, their churches and parents were terribly strict, and you couldn't watch anything without committing a mortal sin . . . well, those days are long gone, my friend. The viewing habits of Christians in the early twenty-first century are generally as loose as those of their secular neighbors, with the possible exception of out-and-out pornography. Just about anything else goes.

This has been true for at least two decades. Chuck Colson tells about attending a dinner in the mid-1980s and sitting next to the president of a major network.

A tremendous opportunity, I thought. I told how millions of Christians were offended by the kind of programming the networks provided.

Knowing TV executives are keenly interested in profit and loss statements, I suggested it would be good business to air wholesome family entertainment. "After all," I said, "there are 50 million born-again Christians out there!"

He looked at me quizzically. I assured him that was Gallup's last figure.

"What you're suggesting, Mr. Colson, is that we run more programs like, say, 'Chariots of Fire'?"

"Yes!" I exclaimed. "That's a great movie with a marvelous Christian message."

"Well," he said, "CBS ran it as a prime-time movie just a few months ago. Are you aware of the ratings?"

All at once I knew I was in trouble.

He then explained: That night NBC showed "On Golden Pond"; it was #1 with 25.2 percent of all TV sets in America tuned in. Close behind was "My Mother's Secret Life," a show about a mother hiding her past as a prostitute. It was #2 with 25.1 percent.

And a distant third—a big money loser—was CBS with "Chariots of Fire"—11.8 percent. In fact, of the 65 shows rated that week . . . "Chariots of Fire" was #57.

"So," my companion concluded, "where are your 50 million born-again Christians, Mr. Colson?"[2]

If Christ is indeed the Lord of all our lives, then we need to "crown him Lord of prime time," as Colson put it at the end of his editorial.

Some Christians rationalize their media choices by saying they need to "keep informed" and "stay up-to-date" on what the general culture is watching. This excuse covers a wide range of contamination. I confess I used to think this way myself. Then one day in my reading I came across Romans 16:19, where the apostle Paul wrote to believers living in the world's epicenter of culture and entertainment, "I want you to be wise about what is good, and innocent about what is evil." He apparently didn't think it was necessary for the Roman Christians to stay current on every detail of what was going on down at the Colosseum, the bathhouses, or the various theaters of the capital city. They had better things with which to fill their minds.

Could it be that what we *see* wields a greater influence than we realize over how we *live*? Week after week spent watching immorality (sugarcoated with humor, of course) can wear down our personal standards of moral behavior. Perhaps there is a connection here with the disappointing statistic from the Barna Research Group that 25 percent of all Americans who call themselves "born again" have cohabited with someone of the opposite sex. The fact that Christian doctrine clearly declares marriage to be the boundary line for sexual intimacy is . . . well, you know, we'll get around to a wedding eventually, and in the meantime, we really do love each other, plus we're saving money, okay?

Granted, the cohabitation statistics for non-Christians are somewhat higher, but not all that much. When one out of every four born-again believers rationalizes this kind of living arrangement, it is a stunning indictment of our discipleship.

Once actually married, with the full blessing of the church, do Christian couples *stay married* longer than their secular counterparts? Having vowed before a holy God to "cleave to each other as long as we both shall live," do we keep that pledge in ways a statistician would notice?

Not really.

Again, the Barna Research numbers, based on a 2004 sampling of 3,614 adults across the nation, are disconcerting:

- Among all adults eighteen and older, three-fourths have been married at least once, half are currently married, and 35 percent have been divorced.
- Among "born-again" adults, four-fifths have been married at least once, a little more than half are currently married—and 35 percent have been divorced. Exactly the same figure as the population at large.

It gets worse. When you look at state-by-state divorce rates, some of the highest numbers are in the Bible Belt. The top ten list includes Arkansas, Alabama, Kentucky, West Virginia, Florida, Tennessee, and Mississippi. By contrast, one of the least church-going states posts the lowest, most admirable number: Massachusetts.[3] What's wrong with this picture?

It is even more embarrassing to look at worldwide statistics and see that the United States, supposedly "a shining city on a hill," leads almost all nations with an annual divorce rate of 4.0 occurrences per one thousand population. Australia and the United Kingdom come in at 2.6, by contrast; France at 2.0; Israel at 1.56; Singapore at 1.31; and our neighbors in Mexico at 0.48. Oh well, at least the Russians are worse than we are, at 4.3.

Jim Cymbala, pastor of the twelve-thousand-strong Brooklyn Tabernacle, says that when he counsels married couples who are fighting with each other, he sometimes feels like saying, "You know, if I were an atheist, I'd ask, 'How come Jesus can't keep you two together?' The fault lies not with Jesus, obviously."

He isn't that blunt, of course. But even softer, more nuanced words go largely unsaid in the current church culture. Says Dr. Barbara Dafoe Whitehead, notable researcher and author of *The Divorce Culture*:

> The debate about divorce and family structure has largely been geared toward baby boomers, many of whom have been divorced. . . . Boomers say, "How dare you criticize my divorce when you don't understand the pain of my decision? You don't understand the reasons I had to do it." . . .
>
> There is a feeling among clergy that to speak frankly about marriage is to be judgmental and unsupportive of all the people sitting in the pews who are divorced. This means those who have the most to say about the commitments of marriage are keeping silent.[4]

This silence comes back to haunt us a second time when the public discourse turns, as is now happening in America, to same-sex marriage. Shouldn't this be permitted in the name of freedom and nondiscrimination? Christians frequently say no, citing not only the prohibitions of Scripture but also claiming that children who grow up in gay unions will be misguided and even at risk of harm.

That quickly leads to the rebuttal of asking about all the children currently suffering the effects of a *conventional* marriage that failed. Said *USA Today* on its editorial page:

> A long line of respected studies on families points to a far more common reason that children increasingly are put at risk: the breakup of heterosexual marriages. . . . Boys raised

in single-parent homes are twice as likely to commit a crime
that leads to prison. . . . Children growing up in single-parent
families are twice as likely to drop out of school. . . .

If [defense-of-marriage] amendment sponsors want to
protect children, as they claim, they can focus more on embracing marriage-building proposals from family experts. . . .
Before they create a coast-to-coast uproar, amendment back-
ers owe the nation proof that the drastic constitutional step
they favor truly would make life better for children.[5]

Without conceding anything on the gay-marriage issue, we
must admit that the swelling tide of kids growing up without
their (straight) dad or (straight) mom is a bad situation,
one that Christians ought to do everything in their power
to prevent. Stable homes give testimony to God's ability to
bend our wills to fit his purposes when he first established
the institution of marriage long ago.

It will require courage for us to shore up this weakness.
It will also take creativity, as well as the investment of time
in more substantial marriage preparation classes, counseling for those couples in difficulty, "in-service" classes and
seminars and retreats and accountability groups . . . useful
formats are abundant.

Furthermore, it will require some of the church's money—
which brings us to another area where practice trails behind
biblical mandate. The giving level in the Protestant world is
currently running at 2.62 percent of members' income—the
lowest rate in thirty-five years. In fact, it's even lower than
what our grandparents were scraping together to give during
the worst of the Great Depression; the giving rate for 1933
was 3.2 percent of income.

So much for the whole "tithing" concept. We're so far from
the 10 percent paradigm that we don't even need to debate
whether tithing is relevant to New Testament Christians

(compared to the Old Testament law). Again, the researchers who study these things report that only 7 percent of today's churchgoers actually tithe.[6]

Meanwhile, the U.S. Department of Transportation now indicates that the average American family has acquired more cars than the number of drivers who live in the home! Average drivers per household: 1.75. Average vehicles per household: 1.9. Hundreds of thousands of consumer products appeal for our discretionary income, and we freely comply, until our homes are packed with "stuff." But when Sunday comes and it's time to give to God's work, many of us hesitate.

Once again, the way we live undermines the credibility of what we say we value. All of this makes for a shaky representation of Christ's plan for this world.

More Than Talk

Along the way, we seem to have somehow missed the steady emphasis in our Lord's ministry on *doing*. It is interesting, when you take in a broad sweep of what Jesus said in the four Gospels, how often he emphasized not just listening to his words but going away and doing them.

One vivid example is the climax to his "Sermon on the Mount." He had spoken with passion and brilliance to the crowds that afternoon. He had started with the Beatitudes, then gone on to contrast what the Law required with what he believed. He had given the magnificent "Lord's Prayer" and invited us all to "ask . . . seek . . . knock." The people sat entranced at his teaching. How would he wrap up this great oration? What would be his grand finale?

He came to his conclusion and, as many speakers do, chose to end with a memorable story. He told about two house builders. They both erected impressive homes. No doubt the neighbors were appreciative of these additions to the community. Both construction projects appeared to be in fine shape.

Then came a downpour of rain that wouldn't stop. The wind blew viciously, and the nearby stream began to flood. Soon the house built on a foundation of sand was in trouble. The house built on rock, meanwhile, didn't budge.

Hmmm . . . what was Jesus's point?

"Therefore everyone who hears these words of mine *and puts them into practice* is like a wise man who built his house on the rock," the Master explained. "But everyone who hears these words of mine and *does not put them into practice* is like a foolish man who built his house on sand" (Matt. 7:24, 26, italic added). In other words, there was no staying power, no endurance, no magic in the talk. Only in the follow-through. Speeches would wash away like loose pebbles. Action put down the necessary roots to stay firm.

That's the kind of viewpoint Jesus held. He hadn't come to earth for just a "speaking tour." He was here to see behavior change.

"Anyone who chooses to *do* the will of God will find out whether my teaching comes from God or whether I speak on my own," he said (John 7:17, italics added).

On his last night with his disciples in the upper room, he stunned them by washing their feet, which led to a riveting discussion about servanthood. Then, having made his case, he landed this closing zinger: "Now that you know these things, you will be blessed if you do them" (John 13:17). An hour or two later, he repeated himself: "You are my friends if you do what I command" (John 15:14).

Early in his ministry, his mother and half-brothers came around to see him in action. They could not get inside the crowded place, however, and a messenger told Jesus about their arrival. He responded with this cryptic comment: "My mother and brothers are those who hear God's word *and put it into practice*" (Luke 8:21, italics added).

Perhaps this was a motif of the family in which Jesus had grown up. Short on talk, long on action. His mother, Mary, is forever remembered for her succinct advice to the waiters at the Cana wedding feast: "Do whatever he tells you" (John 2:5). One of her other sons, James, became a leader in the early church and was known as a man of few words but deep devotion. He wrote one short epistle, which is where we find a forceful bent in the direction of follow-through:

> Do not merely listen to the word, and so deceive yourselves. Do what it says. Those who listen to the word but do not do what it says are like people who look at their faces in a mirror and, after looking at themselves, go away and immediately forget what they look like. But those who look intently into the perfect law that gives freedom and continue in it—not forgetting what they have heard but doing it—they will be blessed in what they do.
>
> James 1:22–24

Simply to look, to observe, to notice . . . but not to act . . . is not just neutral, says this apostle. It is deceptive. You think you're accomplishing something worthy when you're just wasting your time. You've fooled yourself. "I heard a very good sermon today." So what? Did it make any difference in real life? The proof of the preaching is in the living.

James keeps going on this theme in the next chapter.

> What good is it, my brothers and sisters, if people claim to have faith but have no deeds? Can such faith save them? . . . Faith by itself, if it is not accompanied by action, is dead.
>
> James 2:14, 17

Jesus once told a poignant story that every parent can appreciate.

> "What do you think? There was a man who had two sons. He went to the first and said, 'Son, go and work today in the vineyard.'
>
> "'I will not,' he answered, but later he changed his mind and went.
>
> "Then the father went to the other son and said the same thing. He answered, 'I will, sir,' but he did not go.
>
> "Which of the two did what his father wanted?"
>
> "The first," they answered.
>
> Jesus said to them, "Truly I tell you, the tax collectors and the prostitutes are entering the kingdom of God ahead of you."
>
> Matthew 21:28–32

Dr. Tony Campolo, in speaking about this story, calls the first son the kind of child who is "a pain at breakfast, but a joy at supper." He gives his dad grief in the beginning; he's downright exasperating. But eventually, he does the work.

The second son is much more pleasant for starters. He's a smooth fellow who always has the right words. Only later do we learn that he is "a joy at breakfast, but a pain at supper," says Campolo.

The point is that talk is cheap; action is what counts. The Christian life is more than a matter of right talking and right doctrine. It is *right demonstration*. That is what cuts ice with a watching world. They really don't care all that much about what we believe. They are impressed instead with how we live.

The apostle Paul worried in Romans 2 about the gap between profession and follow-through. He asked his fellow Jews whether they were in fact keeping the law they proclaimed. If not, he said, "As it is written: 'God's name is blasphemed among the Gentiles because of you'" (v. 24).

When we don't live the way we profess, it triggers cynicism and reproach—"blasphemy"—among outsiders to the faith. It undercuts the cause. We simply cannot endure as a generation of speakers and hearers. When words become an end in themselves, an elegant pageantry for us to indulge in our sanctuaries, our books, our concerts, and our programs, they are useless. Words are instead to be the means for implementing God's intentions in a dark world. That is what our neighbors and acquaintances are waiting to see.

Part Three

Envoys of Heaven

9

Peace on the Inside

Before we delve into the many things we might *do* to help God's cause in the world, let us spend one chapter thinking about what and who we *are*.

When an essay contest was announced in Great Britain to address the topic "What is wrong with the world?" the brilliant G. K. Chesterton (1874–1936) submitted a very short entry. This eloquent author, whose works influenced the young C. S. Lewis toward Christianity, sent in just two words. The answer to the question, wrote Chesterton, was this: "I am!"

Thus with impeccable wit he owned up to the fact that the world's difficulties are not so much "out there" as they are internal to us as human beings. The same can be said of the institutional church. While it is much easier to blame external forces for the difficulties we face, a more useful approach is to look inward.

God, in appointing us as his ambassadors, knew in the beginning that we would not do a perfect job. He was fully aware of our shortcomings. The foibles and embarrassments outlined in the preceding three chapters have not caught him off-guard. The amazing thing, I suppose, is that we ambassadors have not yet been fired. God shows a spectacular measure of grace and longsuffering in keeping us employed as his envoys.

No doubt he wants us to serve his purposes better in the future, however. The starting point toward that goal is to examine our hearts, before our actions.

The Jesus Style

When Jesus sent out his emissaries for short ministry tours, he instructed them not only on what to do in public venues but also how to conduct themselves in private homes. "When you enter a house, first say, 'Peace to this house.' If the head of the house loves peace, your peace will rest on that house; if not, it will return to you" (Luke 10:5–6). This directive, given to the seventy-two, is almost exactly the same as that given earlier to the twelve when they went out (Matt. 10:12–13).

What is this "peace" that Jesus seems to think can be dispensed into an environment almost like a vibration or a pleasant fragrance? And how would the disciples know whether or not their "peace" had been welcomed?

Apparently Jesus felt that when these representatives left his presence to head into the world at large, they carried with them not only words to explain the good news of the kingdom of heaven, power to heal the sick, even authority to cast out demons . . . but also an invisible tranquility, a sense of calm, to soothe whatever troubled situation they encountered. In some places, their peaceful influence would be embraced; in others, it would be rebuffed, like same-pole magnet ends pushing each other away. The traveling ministers were told to take notice of which was which.

In no case were they told to stir up animosity or contention as they traveled. Granted, this sometimes happened on its own throughout early church history in spite of their best efforts. But as far as Christ was concerned, his agents were to transmit a peaceful influence.

Early in his ministry, he had declared, "Blessed are the peacemakers, for they will be called children of God" (Matt. 5:9). Before he was even born in the Bethlehem stable, the aged Zechariah prophesied that he would "guide our feet into the path of peace" (Luke 1:79). Jesus instructed his disciples to "be at peace with each other" (Mark 9:50), a theme repeated by Paul in 1 Thessalonians 5:13–14, "Live in peace with each other. And we urge you, brothers and sisters, warn those who are idle and disruptive, encourage the disheartened, help the weak, be patient with everyone."

When the U.S. State Department is choosing a person to represent the nation in a foreign embassy, they are not looking for a chronic troublemaker or pot-stirrer. They are looking instead for someone who fundamentally, constitutionally tends in the direction of working out problems rather than igniting them, someone who would rather pour oil on the waters than churn them into a froth. This ability to get along has its foundation in the person's internal disposition. Barging into showdowns and head-butting is not their idea of fun.

The same should be true of us, if indeed the fruit of the Holy Spirit is growing in our hearts. Third in that well-known list in Galatians 5 is "peace." Fourth is "patience." Fifth is "kindness." Eighth is "gentleness." Ninth is "self-control" (v.

23). The rest of the paragraph talks about crucifying our "passions and desires" (v. 24) and "not . . . provoking and envying each other" (v. 26).

The heart and soul that is at rest in Christ is the one prepared to represent him well in today's world. Attempts by others to rile, to incite, to inflame will be doused with the calming love of God. We all live in a modern climate bent on agitation. From crowded freeways to aggressive business competitors to political debates, our society throbs with turbulence. To resist this constant baiting requires a deep peace on the inside.

Early in our married life, my wife and I found ourselves in a troubled season. I was pursuing a master's degree while she supported us with a teaching job nearly twenty miles away. That particular winter turned out to be one of the snowiest on record in upstate New York. Commuting was a real strain in her life. On top of this, we lived in a small second-floor apartment directly above a would-be opera singer who invariably began her practicing around eleven o'clock at night. We found ourselves growing more and more tense as the weeks wore on.

"Maybe we should start a Bible study together," my wife said one day, "on what the Bible says about *peace*. We could certainly use some, don't you think?" I heartily agreed.

More than thirty years later, we still cherish the page of our handwritten notes. After reading John 14:23–31 we recorded that "Peace is a real *something* that Christ deposits" in his people. Isaiah 9:6–7 reminded us that the coming Messiah was "the source of an infinite peace that *increases, expands* in our individual situations." Psalm 29 taught us that "peace is a state of mind *within* action." Second Timothy 2:22 and Romans 14:19 told us to "follow after—aim at peace. The human initiative is needed too." Isaiah 26:3 and following said that if we "take charge mentally, and concentrate on the LORD, peace will result." These and other Scriptures spoke to our deep agitation.

As a result of this study, we both became more serene. The snowstorms didn't let up, and the piercing soprano arias didn't go away . . . but we were more composed on the inside; we drew upon the peace of God. We learned that he could implant within us an antidote to the clamor of our living situation.

The prophet said, "In repentance and rest is your salvation, in quietness and trust is your strength" (Isa. 30:15). This noisy world will never foster the kind of strength we need. God's still small voice can be heard only when we quiet down and listen to his eternal wisdom.

Be Still and Know

The full portion of peace that ambassadors need is not likely to be sustained amid hectic schedules and constant interaction with other people. Every morning we wake up to face a day already crammed with appointments, phone calls, emails, news reports, and friends eager to speak with us. These things, however, have a way of making us more distracted than focused.

In solitude we find the time and ability to compose ourselves, to center our thoughts on Christ, and to regain our sense of peace. Yes, it's very hard to make this time in our busy lives. But that does not mean it is optional for us. As President Dwight Eisenhower wisely put it, "The urgent problems are seldom the important ones." The importance of being alone cannot be overstated.

Consider the example of Moses, prince of Egypt. He was destined for greatness, but in an explosive moment, he ruined everything by killing an Egyptian slavemaster who was abusing an Israelite worker. Moses ran in a panic for the border.

The next time he set foot inside of Egypt, he had spent an awful lot of time alone in the desert, tending sheep. He had taken time to know himself—his strengths, his weaknesses, his need for self-control. God had met with him there. At last, God commissioned him to return to the scene of his earlier fiasco and be the mastermind of a dramatic liberation.

Things now got very noisy. The pharaoh had much to say to him. Even the elders of Israel threw in their two cents from time to time. Moses remained unshakable. He kept his eye on the goal and never flinched in the face of pressure. He was a man at peace with himself and in tune with Jehovah. Come what may—plagues, entrapment at the Red Sea, even followers who complained—Moses was equal to the task. His character had been steeled in the desert alone.

In Henri Nouwen's book *The Way of the Heart*, he unfolded what it is like to undergo this kind of training.

> In solitude I get rid of my scaffolding: no friends to talk with, no telephone calls to make, no meetings to attend, no music to entertain, no books to distract, just me—naked, vulnerable, weak, sinful, broken—nothing. It is this nothingness that I have to face in my solitude, a nothingness so dreadful that everything in me wants to run to my friends, my work, and my distractions so that I can forget my nothingness and make myself believe that I am worth something. But that is not all. As soon as I decide to stay in my solitude, confusing ideas, disturbing images, wild fantasies, and weird associations jump about in my mind like monkeys in a banana tree.

Yes, indeed. All of us can appreciate what Nouwen says here. It is not easy to break away from our routines and be content in aloneness. However, as he continues:

We are . . . not completely alone. Christ is with us. . . .

Our primary task in solitude . . . is not to pay undue attention to the many faces which assail us, but to keep the eyes of our mind and heart on him who is our divine Savior. Only in the context of grace can we face our sin; only in the place of healing do we dare to show our wounds; only with a single-minded attention to Christ can we give up our clinging fears and face our own true nature. . . .

Solitude is thus the place of purification and transformation, the place of the great struggle and the great encounter. . . . It is the place where Christ remodels us in his own image and frees us from the victimizing compulsions of the world.[1]

I recognize that some people are more comfortable with solitude than others. Some do not mind having a half-day or even a full day of quietness, while others are frustrated within thirty minutes. All of us, regardless of temperament, will eventually grow uneasy and wish for a familiar distraction: the shopping mall, the TV, the phone. It does not hurt any of us to say no to these things and remain in the presence of the One who has far more important things to say to us.

The writer of Hebrews talks about "the promise of entering his rest" (4:1) and frankly admits that, as good as that sounds, it doesn't come without a push. "Let us, therefore, make every effort to enter that rest, so that no one will perish" (4:11). *Make an effort* to rest? That doesn't seem logical, does it? Is not rest the absence of effort or exertion? Yes—but to get to that state frequently means pushing our driven personalities against their natural grain. It takes *work* to make ourselves slow down and hear the voice of God.

As a child, I had the advantage (although I didn't think so at the time) of being raised by parents who thought silence and solitude were good things. One of the memory verses they assigned to me was Lamentations 3:27–28 (King James Version, of course, in those days): "It is good for a man that he bear the yoke in his youth. He sitteth alone and keepeth silence, because he hath borne it upon him." I can remember times of asking permission to go across the street and play with my friend Kent, only to be told, "No, not today. You need some time just to wind down."

"Why, Mom?" I would protest. "We're not gonna get in any trouble—I promise."

She would faintly smile but then turn back to whatever she was doing without a further word. I knew her decision would stand.

Now as an adult I look back and grudgingly give her the benefit of the doubt. There's merit in even an energetic boy spending time alone.

After all, the Son of God during his time on earth was known to disappear occasionally in order to engage in serious prayer. Disciples would be mystified—*where did he go?!*—and search until they found him. He was simply restoring his inner strength by communicating with his heavenly Father.

I once had the privilege to interview one of the great minds of the twentieth century, the Quaker philosopher and author D. Elton Trueblood. He was then in his mid-eighties, retired from many of his earlier obligations, so that time was plentiful in his life. Yet he set the interview for 9:00 a.m. and let me know in advance that it would be ending promptly at 10:30. That led to a conversation about scheduling and time allocation. Dr. Trueblood said with the wisdom of a sage: "He who is always available is not worth enough when he *is* available."

To be envoys of value to God means that we need to govern our time in such a way that our peaceful center remains undisturbed. The individual patterns and rhythms are up to each person to set, of course. But the objective must never be compromised. "The peace of God, which transcends all understanding" must have adequate opportunity to "guard your hearts and your minds in Christ Jesus" (Phil. 4:7).

When Peace Is Tested

The benefits of alone time in our work as representatives of Christ may not be always apparent. But the day will come when the pressure is on, and outside observers will notice something different about the Christian, a unique composure not common to the average person.

A number of years ago, in the central African nation now called the Democratic Republic of the Congo, a huge rally occurred in the soccer stadium at Matadi to mark the centennial of Swedish Covenant missionary effort in that region. Some one hundred thousand Christians gathered for the all-day event. Congolese pastors spoke about the coming of the gospel and what a change it had made in their society. Musicians sang, and food was shared among the massive crowd. The atmosphere was festive.

Then late in the afternoon, an aged man with a cane came forward asking to speak. His name was not on the program. He persuaded the moderator to give him time regardless.

"There is something I have to tell you all," he said as he took the microphone. "I will soon die, and if I do not tell you what occurred, the information will go to my grave with me.

"When I was a very little boy, I heard the story of the white people's arrival from Sweden. We thought at first they were ghosts, because of their white skin. My parents and the others of that generation found them very strange. They spoke of many things about God that we had never heard before. They claimed to know the way to heaven; they said anyone could be sure of coming to rest in peace with God at the end of life.

"The elders of our tribe were unsure about whether to allow these ideas to stay in our villages or not. They met together in council and decided upon a test. They would arrange to poison the missionaries slowly by tampering with their food. Then we would see how their beliefs endured or not.

"One by one, they died—men, women, children. When one would die, their family members would grieve as they buried them, of course. But they did not waver in their faith.

"And then, new people would arrive from their country with the same message that God loves us. Finally, the elders accepted that these were real people, in spite of their color and their ideas. It was decided to stop poisoning them.

"Every member of the tribe was sworn to secrecy. The truth has stayed hidden now for almost one hundred years. I am the last one living who knew of this. I am a witness. They came to tell us the truth, that God loves us."

These missionaries' fortitude, even in the midst of personal anguish, had sent a powerful message to everyone who watched them. The result of this early sacrifice was now evident to all.

When I heard that story, I could not help noting that those early pioneers *never knew what was really going on*. They assumed they had simply contracted some mysterious tropical disease that cut them down without mercy. Their relatives back home never dreamed that they had been consciously targeted for a test of faith.

We never know who is watching us. We seldom see the full picture. We are simply called to be good and faithful servants of the Lord Almighty, whose kingdom is ordained to prevail. As we give evidence of his stability in our own lives, through pleasant times and dreadful times, the truth of his Word is noticed by others. The gospel goes forward. This is our ultimate goal, and our reward.

10

Bridge Building

It's fairly easy for critics to portray religion as an agitator in the world. All they have to do is start telling stories of the Crusades, the Spanish Inquisition, the "Troubles" of Northern Ireland, the various jihadist movements of Islam, or any similar conflict. If humanity were not so inflamed with religious passion, they argue, there would be far less anguish and bloodshed.

On the other hand, an equal number of examples could be cited of Christian voices serving to *calm* inflammatory situations, to work for fairness and understanding. Some examples take place on the world stage, while others happen in tiny villages and even within families, where they draw little notice. One of the most dramatic stories of a calming Christian presence in recent times was the intervention of godly, praying leaders when South Africa was about to explode in the early 1990s. Michael Cassidy, founder and president of African Enterprise, and a white South African himself, tells the story in his book *A Witness For Ever.*

Here was a nation of forty million people "on a knife-edge," he writes, after half a century of apartheid. The black majority had suffered a mountain of indignities and were at a point of understandable fury, while the white minority fretted behind high gates and feared for their lives. Civil war seemed inevitable. Unemployment stood above 50 percent, due in part to worldwide sanctions. At least eight different political parties and movements pushed to have their way. One of their leaders was quoted as saying, "We must get used to the smell of blood." The ominous slogan was bandied about, "One settler, one bullet," meaning that only when the white population was entirely slaughtered would there be peace. After the Rodney King riots in America in 1992, one South African politician announced, "We are quite capable of reproducing the Los Angeles scenes here in Pietermaritzburg." In fact, such scenes were already happening in scattered townships and cities.

Some people on both sides of the racial divide professed Christian loyalty but could not seem to translate that into a workable plan for the future. Others had been driven away entirely. Said John Nkadimeng, member of the African National Congress (ANC) executive board, "I came out of a tribal background and because of what some white Christians did to us in the Northern Transvaal, I came to hate Christianity. Those people drove me to explore Karl Marx and I joined the South African Communist Party."[1] His story was not unusual.

In the midst of this tinderbox, Cassidy and his associates began asking what they might do in the name of Christ to rescue their beloved country. They pondered ways in which their evangelistic organization, with its network of friends in many other African nations that had already transitioned to majority rule, could have an influence. In connection with an upcoming conference, Cassidy invited seven teams from such diverse places as Uganda, Zimbabwe, and Kenya to stay an extra two weeks to simply make visits to various national leaders. They would not lobby or give political advice; they would only tell their stories and offer to pray for their hosts. The stories, of course, included how Christ had helped them forgive the insults they had endured in their own countries.

John Gatu of Kenya and a Tanzanian bishop sat down with Dr. Andries Treurnicht, leader of the Conservative Party and viewed as South Africa's most notorious white supremacist.

> [Gatu] told Dr. Treurnicht that years previously he had been caught up in the Mau Mau movement and had hated whites with a passion. But then he had been converted to Christ. His heart began to change and this hatred diminished dramatically. . . . [Eventually, he said,] "I have to say to you that, although I do not agree with your politics at all . . . I want to ask you for your forgiveness. While I may not like someone's views, my Bible does not allow me to be bitter towards that person. I therefore want to give you the right hand of fellowship and greet you as my brother."
>
> At this he stood and held out his right hand to grasp the hesitating hand of Dr. Treurnicht, whose previously startled eyes were now filled with tears.
>
> "Nothing like that has ever happened to me before," said Treurnicht.[2]

The result of this two-week appointment blitz—201 meetings in all—was a thaw in hostilities, to the point that a few months later, African Enterprise was able to begin hosting weekend retreats at a wild-game lodge north of Pretoria. National leaders both black and white were willing to come and at least listen to one another. They heard each other's autobiographies, sometimes shuddering at the painful abuses endured during imprisonments. They shared their vision for a new South Africa that would be nonracial in its structure. All kinds of myths and assumptions were laid aside as powerful men and women got to know each other personally.

This kind of dialogue in 1992 played a strategic role in forwarding the chance for national elections in which *everyone* could vote, slated for April 27, 1994. Prayer meetings were organized across the nation to implore God's help. Most people assumed that Nelson Mandela of the ANC would win the presidency; the trick was to assure the other groups that they would not be slighted by the new government. Tensions continued to run high as the election approached.

The three-million-member Zulu tribe, with its Inkatha Freedom Party (IFP), was especially on edge; they threatened to boycott the election and set up a separate nation. That would almost surely plunge the region into a bloodbath. The most prestigious negotiators the outside world could offer—Henry Kissinger of the U.S. and Lord Carrington, former foreign secretary of the U.K.—arrived to try to help. Meetings ran long into the night. The clock kept ticking.

To the dismay of everyone, no resolution could be found. Kissinger confided to a friend, "I have never been on such a catastrophic mission, and its failure now has cataclysmic consequences for South Africa." He and Carrington boarded their planes at Johannesburg's airport and departed, leaving all sides in despair. The London *Sunday Times* called it all "a bloody mess."

107

It was at this grim moment that Michael Cassidy's longtime friend, a godly professor from Kenya named Washington Okumu, went to work on his own. Meeting with first one faction, then another, then another, he crafted a compromise to keep the IFP in the election while not threatening the ANC's dominance or frightening off the white groups' participation. A special role for the Zulu king would be arranged, but without derailing the democratic principle. Okumu shuttled from city to city, touching base with everyone from President F. W. de Klerk to Nelson Mandela to Chief Buthelezi to the head of the election commission, who faced the logistical nightmare of adjusting millions of paper ballots at the last minute.

Meanwhile, that Sunday in Durban, Cassidy spoke to more than twenty thousand people at a Jesus Peace Rally:

> Our summits have failed, our international mediators have gone home shattered, our politicians are at their wits' end, and it would seem almost impossible to pull off a free and fair election. . . . This is a moment of human extremity. But man's extremity is God's opportunity.
>
> In Scripture this is seen in many places in the two titanic little words: "Then Jesus. . . ." In the power of the crucified and risen Christ stands the power we need in South Africa at this time. . . .
>
> Lord, we have sought to do our part. Won't you now, supernaturally, overwhelmingly, overpoweringly, do yours?[3]

By Tuesday noon, all the principal leaders had agreed to Okumu's plan. The nation breathed a corporate sigh of relief. The elections scheduled for one week later could proceed after all, with full participation.

And thus South Africa emerged into the sunshine at last.

The *Boston Globe* reported, "Faith had role in apartheid's end." The *Daily News of Durban* headline read, "How God stepped in to save South Africa." *Time* magazine admitted, "History has thrown up an authentic miracle." John Simpson of the BBC put it this way: "It was the Jesus Peace Rally which tipped the scales."[4]

Reconcilers

This is a classic example of what 2 Corinthians 5:18 calls "the ministry of reconciliation," which we highlighted in chapter 2 of this book. God's ambassadors in the world are meant to have a calming effect on the complex and often fractious arena of human relationships. Whenever people are at one another's throats—internationally, nationally, locally, in the family—God is grieved. This is not the world he intended in the beginning, and humanity's constant wrangling and contention is not something he easily accepts. He is innately a God of *shalom*—peace, wholeness, contentment.

If you and I indeed "participate in the divine nature, having escaped the corruption in the world caused by evil desires" (2 Peter 1:4), then we're on his side in this regard. We're on the peacemaking team. We're the people, perhaps few in number but determined nevertheless, who smooth out the bumps in human interaction.

We're not to be like the disciples who, when treated coldly by a certain Samaritan village, thought it might be a good idea to pull an Elijah redux and call down fire from heaven. They'd teach these scoundrels a quick lesson. Enough of this disrespect!

Jesus did not agree with the disciples at all. "He turned, and rebuked them," the King James Version records, "and said, Ye know not what manner of spirit ye are of. For the

Son of man is not come to destroy men's lives, but to save them" (Luke 9:55–56).

This quotation does not appear in the most reliable New Testament manuscripts (and thus not in most modern translations, except as a footnote)—but I can well imagine Jesus saying this kind of thing. It would be good for us, his modern followers, to ask ourselves: What "manner of spirit" are we carrying around, anyway? A spirit that escalates conflict and misunderstanding, or a spirit that tries to reduce them? How are we "pre-wired" in this area? And do we need to change the wiring?

The apostle Paul, who had been something of a hothead in his early days, vigorously organizing SWAT teams to barge into Christian homes and meetings, eventually wrote to the Roman believers: "If it is possible, as far as it depends on you, live at peace with everyone. Do not take revenge, my dear friends, but leave room for God's wrath. . . . Do not be overcome by evil, but overcome evil with good" (12:18–19, 21). He was realistic enough to admit that sometimes peace is not "possible." Of two (or more) people involved in a dispute, perhaps one is simply intractable. But "as far as it depends on you," he writes, you can work toward a peaceful resolution.

It will not necessarily be easy. But it can reap surprising rewards. Says James, "The wisdom that comes from heaven is first of all pure; then peace-loving, considerate, submissive, full of mercy and good fruit, impartial and sincere. Peacemakers who sow in peace reap a harvest of righteousness" (3:17–18).

"Something Divine"

Part of that harvest is a favorable impression among unbelievers who notice the Christian way at work. In the early part of the second century AD, when the church was being viciously persecuted and maligned throughout the Roman empire, an Athenian orator named Aristides sent a surprising report to the emperor Hadrian. Aristides had been quietly observing how Christians actually lived and related to others. He wrote at some length:

> The Christians . . . placate those who oppress them and make them their friends; they do good to their enemies. Their wives are absolutely pure, and their daughters modest. Their men abstain from unlawful marriage and from all impurity. If any of them have bondwomen or children, they persuade them to become Christians for the love they have toward them; and when they become so, they call them without distinction "brothers". . . .
>
> They love one another. They do not refuse to help the widows. They rescue the orphan from him who does him violence. He who has gives ungrudgingly to him who has not. If they see a stranger, they take him to their dwellings and rejoice over him as over a real brother; for they do not call themselves brothers after the flesh, but after the Spirit and in God. . . .
>
> If anyone among them is poor and needy, and they do not have food to spare, they fast for two or three days, that they may supply him with necessary food. . . .
>
> Because of them there flows forth all the beauty that there is in the world. But the good deeds they do they do not proclaim in the ears of the multitude, but they take care that no one shall perceive them. Thus they labor to become righteous. . . .
>
> Truly, this is a new people and there is something divine in them.[5]

What a wonderful overview. The sum total of gracious living and relating among the Christian community swept

111

up this observer to the point of attributing to them "all the beauty that there is in the world." Perhaps he exaggerated a bit—but what an endorsement.

Aristides perhaps said more than he knew when he concluded that "there is something divine in them." Indeed there was. It was called the love of God.

When the love, compassion, and gentleness of Jesus Christ live inside us, it makes a huge difference in our external relationships. We are not easily offended. We are not quick to condemn or antagonize. We are instead the kind of people to whom others are drawn, whatever their stated worldview.

Several years ago, I was speaking at a Chicago church and met a young woman named Ginger who worked in the advertising industry. She asked me some questions about the publishing field, saying she hoped to write a book. I tried to be honest in replying that the odds for any first-time author to be published are quite dismal, but if she had a good idea, she should definitely pursue it. I gave her a few contact names to try.

She did manage to catch a publisher's attention, and in time I received a copy of her book in the mail, along with a thank-you note. Only upon reading it did I learn how Ginger had come to Christ in the first place. She wrote that she had grown up in a typical Christian family, going to church each week because her parents said so, but never really feeling drawn toward the faith. Eventually she went off to Michigan State University and dismissed the religion thing quite thoroughly.

But then . . .

During my senior year . . . only weeks before I was to graduate, I found myself in trouble and was about to be thrown off campus. I had hosted a party in the dormitory that I, uh, really shouldn't have. Everyone short of the dorm director was there. Alcohol was flowing freely and the party was in full swing—until the dorm director showed up. As I faced suspension, I feared the worst.

But someone stepped in and went to bat for me: an optimistic young lady who was nothing at all like me. She didn't drink, didn't smoke, didn't swear, didn't consume any of the things I lived for. She even ate the dorm food without complaining! She was my resident hall assistant and she was a Christian. . . .

As she reviewed with me the university policy regarding parties, as well as the dangers of drinking, not once did she berate or belittle me. There was something genuinely different about her. She always seemed happy without indulging in the vices common to college students. Her happiness was founded in her relationship with Christ and she didn't get in the way of allowing others to see it. There were no tracts slipped under my door; her testimony was in her actions.

She didn't judge me. In fact, she saved my neck, preventing my suspension. . . .

I didn't know my resident hall assistant well, but I knew that I wanted what she had. Not needed, but wanted. That's when I first craved the Lord.[6]

Ginger did not deserve a favor from this dorm assistant. Her behavior had violated university rules, not to mention moral considerations. Yet the Christian young woman sensed that a little mercy might go a long way in this case toward reversing Ginger's reckless lifestyle. Like Jesus with the guilty woman in John 8, she read the situation sensitively and opted for the approach of "Go and sin no more." The result was a life drawn in the direction of the Savior, an adulthood rescued.

This is what good diplomats do: they see the greater good that can be realized with just a little nuance. As diplomats of heaven, our task is to represent God's highest interest, which is bringing human beings to himself. How we handle ourselves in the middle of sticky relationships has a lot to do with success versus failure in this effort.

Cleaning Our Own House

When our own relationships within the Christian community do not provide the best model to observers, we owe it to God and ourselves to do something about it. Paul wrote with some irritation to the Corinthian believers about their internal disputes winding up in court, for example. "Do you ask for a ruling from those whose way of life is scorned in the church? I say this to shame you. Is it possible that there is nobody among you wise enough to judge a dispute between believers? But instead, one brother goes to law against another—and this in front of unbelievers!" (1 Cor. 6:4–6).

This passage is brushed aside all too frequently in today's Christian community. Church groups sue each other; publishers, authors, musicians, and other parachurch folks keep the lawyers busy, it seems. It creates a terrible impression among outside observers who had assumed we were followers of the Prince of Peace.

In chapter 8 I wrote about the less-than-stellar marriage statistics for "born-again" Americans. Are we going to do anything about this? Or are we just going to sigh in resignation, as if the matter is insoluble?

Pastors in a number of cities have, in recent years, tightened up their requirements for couples seeking to be married. They have begun insisting upon a certain amount of premarital instruction. Some star-struck couples, in fact, come to realize they shouldn't get married after all. Since the mid-1980s, syndicated columnist Mike McManus has been lobbying pastors to implement a "Community Marriage

Policy," whereby they pledge together in writing that their churches will be more than "wedding factories." They will make sure the marriages they perform have a reasonable chance of enduring, and impatient couples who don't like the requirements at one church will get no quicker service down the street.

Clergy in 183 different cities across 40 states have signed this pledge, cutting local divorce rates in half as a result.[7] The program has been featured on ABC's *World News Tonight*, *NBC Nightly News*, CBS's *48 Hours*, MSNBC, *Oprah*, PBS (twice), as well as in *Time*, *Newsweek*, and hundreds of newspapers.

Concerned Christians in the political arena have also gotten busy. Three states with worse-than-average divorce rates (Louisiana, Arkansas, Arizona) have installed a "covenant marriage" option, whereby couples can deliberately make divorce harder to enact. The Arkansas Act 1486 of 2001, for example, says that if you choose a Covenant Marriage, you agree that:

- You will go to premarital counseling before applying for a marriage license.
- After the wedding, if your marriage seems to be in trouble, you will seek counseling before pursuing divorce.
- You will not file for divorce until after a "cooling-off" separation of two years (two and a half years if children are present) that, hopefully, will result in reconciliation.
- The only admissible grounds for divorce will be adultery, commission of a felony, or physical or sexual abuse. In other words, "incompatibility" and other such rationales don't cut it. The whole "no-fault" concept is abandoned. (Legal separation is allowed in cases of "habitual drunkenness for one year, cruel and barba-

rous treatment, or such indignities as to render the spouse's condition intolerable.")[8]

Arkansas couples who were already married before the law passed can go to the county clerk's office and convert their conventional union to a Covenant Marriage. In fact, that's what the governor and his wife, Mike and Janet Huckabee, did in front of 6,400 people at a Valentine's Day 2005 event at a North Little Rock sports arena. Married some thirty years, they repeated their vows in front of Dennis Rainey, president of FamilyLife (a Campus Crusade division), and then led thousands of other couples that night to do the same.

Huckabee, a Baptist minister, explained that the legal option was meant to "just put some speed bumps in the way, to make us stop and think how important it is that we stay together, how much we have invested in this marriage, and how much would be lost if somehow either one of us or both of us decided to walk away from it."[9]

A few protesters held signs outside the arena, of course, claiming Arkansas was promoting a Christian agenda and discriminating against gay couples. The governor clarified that private donations had picked up most of the tab for the evening, and added, "If taxpayers understood how much divorce costs the state, they'd be begging us to spend some more money holding them together."[10]

Some Arkansas churches have now decided to offer engaged couples the Covenant Marriage format only, seeing it as closer to the God-ordained model than the bare-minimum approach that society has invented.

These and other steps indicate to all who care to notice that Christians take relationships seriously. Marriage and family life is one arena where we can demonstrate this. The workplace is another. The neighborhood is another. Political life is yet another, ranging from the local level up through the state or province, on to the nation, and then even to the international scene.

Healing and sustaining the bonds of human contact is part of God's work in the world. "Let your gentleness be evident to all," the apostle exhorted. "The Lord is near" (Phil. 4:5). He is ever watching how we get along with one another. He is monitoring our interactions. He notices when we build bridges and when we blow them up.

As representatives of a higher kingdom based on love, we are called to lead the way in the pursuit of *shalom*.

11

One-Way Kindness

While harmonious relationships are vital to our Christian witness, we have yet another bridge to cross. It has to do with how we treat people who are outside our normal circles.

Jesus talked about that once in a fairly shocking manner. On a particular Sabbath day, he was the dinner guest of a prominent Pharisee. No doubt the best food had been prepared and brought to a beautiful table. The atmosphere carried an elegance that befitted the upper class. Polite conversation ensued about various topics of the day. Oil lamps lent a soft glow to the room. Waiters stood at attention in the shadows, ready to step quickly to meet the smallest need for more water or a utensil.

Then in the midst of this pleasant ambience . . .

Jesus said to his host, "When you give a luncheon or dinner, do not invite your friends, your brothers or sisters, your relatives, or your rich neighbors. If you do, they may invite you back and so you will be repaid. But when you give a banquet, invite the poor, the crippled, the lame, the blind, and you will be blessed. Although they cannot repay you, you will be repaid at the resurrection of the righteous."

Luke 14:12–14

I'm sure the other guests looked down at their plates and said to themselves, *He's kidding, right?* My goodness—what was this young rabbi from Nazareth trying to imply?! Did he not appreciate the quality of the present company? Did he want some of them to leave? What an awkward moment.

The Bible says one brave fellow tried to make amends and ease the tension in the room by recasting what Jesus had said in a more theoretical tone. Perhaps the conversation could move along quickly now to a heavenly scenario. . . .

When one of those at the table with him heard this, he said to Jesus, "Blessed are those who will eat at the feast in the kingdom of God."

Luke 14:15

It didn't work. Jesus immediately jumped back to the present with an even more detailed response—a parable about a man throwing a big banquet who was snubbed by various invitees who thought up lame excuses about schedule conflicts. They said they needed to go look at real estate . . . check out some cattle . . . stay home with their new bride for some cuddle time. In the end, the frustrated man filled up his banquet tables with, again, "the poor, the crippled, the blind and the lame" (Luke 14:21), even if this meant his servant had to go out into the streets and pull them in by the elbow.

119

Didn't Jesus understand that a core premise of social inter-action and hospitality is *reciprocity?* I invite you to my house or apartment, and then you return the favor by inviting me to yours. This keeps the relationship on an even keel. Neither of us feels beholden to the other. We are equals. When Christmas comes around, I will give you a modest gift to wish you well during the holidays, and you will give me something similar (but not identical, you understand) in order to keep the scales balanced.

Yet here comes the Son of God upsetting social decorum. He wants us to extend hospitality and graciousness to *those who cannot reciprocate.* He thinks this would be an excellent thing to do. Go ahead and get out the china and crystal, he says, for people who have been eating out of dumpsters. Spread the linen tablecloth for those wearing rags. Welcome into your well-decorated home those who have no eyesight with which to appreciate its beauty.

A Reason to Be Different

Whatever excuses we might muster to sidestep this kind of activity, we do have to admit it would draw attention. Needy people whom life has scorned would be most surprised. And others, watching from the sidelines, would be impressed with the notion that God truly cares about the have-nots of the world. Furthermore, his people care too.

They might watch for a while to see what indirect payback we're seeking: a tax deduction, perhaps, or our names in the newspaper, or some other benefit. If these are in fact our motive, the lesson will be lost. But if over time we seek to lift up the destitute and broken simply because they are in pain (physical or otherwise), skeptical onlookers will say to themselves, *Wow—that's different.*

Think for a moment about the public image of the Christian group known as the Salvation Army. People from all walks of life and all religious beliefs (or none) say good things about them as they observe their homeless shelters, addiction treatment programs, food and blankets for those hit by hurricanes and fires, care for abandoned children, and numerous other good works in 109 nations of the world. Nonbelievers and secular corporations even give major amounts of money to help this organization's work go forward.

The goodwill is certainly not because of the odd-sounding brand name. Few people in the Western world these days would say they want "salvation," especially not from some kind of religious "army." The early cadres of General William and Catherine Booth's group were heckled for this identity, to be sure. But now we've grown accustomed to the moniker. However, what if we heard of a new group called the "Holiness Battalion" or the "Sanctification Brigade"? We would not go running in their direction . . . unless we came to know their compassionate heart. Once we saw love in action, we'd forget about the label.

One-way kindness is a way God catches the cynic off-guard. It wordlessly demonstrates the gospel, the Good News that God himself reached out to all of humanity though we had no value to give in return. He sent his Son to help us. When God's people do the same for desperate people in their world, the gospel is reenacted for modern observers.

The Scripture could not be clearer about this priority. Both Old and New Testaments say in no uncertain terms how God feels about the poor. Here is just a sampling:

> If anyone is poor among your people in any of the towns of the land that the LORD your God is giving you, do not be hardhearted or tightfisted toward them. Rather, be open-

handed and freely lend them whatever they need. . . . Give generously to them and do so without a grudging heart.

Deuteronomy 15:7–8, 10

Whoever mocks the poor shows contempt for their Maker.

Proverbs 17:5

Those who are kind to the poor lend to the LORD, and he will reward them for what they have done.

Proverbs 19:17

Those who shut their ears to the cry of the poor will also cry out and not be answered.

Proverbs 21:13

The generous will themselves be blessed.

Proverbs 22:9

Those who give to the poor will lack nothing, but those who close their eyes to them receive many curses.

Proverbs 28:27

Share with the Lord's people who are in need. Practice hospitality.

Romans 12:13

Macedonia and Achaia were pleased to make a contribution for the poor among the Lord's people in Jerusalem. They were pleased to do it, and indeed they owe it to them.

Romans 15:26–27

[Following a description about a major doctrinal dispute in the early church:] All they asked was that we should continue to remember the poor, the very thing I had been eager to do all along (Gal. 2:10). [In other words, "We may not agree on a number of other issues, but when it comes to helping the poor, there's no need for debate. We all just do it."]

As we have opportunity, let us do good to all people, especially to those who belong to the family of believers.

Galatians 6:10

Religion that God our Father accepts as pure and faultless is this: to look after orphans and widows in their distress.

James 1:27

Listen, my dear brothers and sisters: Has not God chosen those who are poor in the eyes of the world to be rich in faith and to inherit the kingdom he promised those who love him?

James 2:5

Faith by itself, if it is not accompanied by action, is dead.

James 2:17

As much as we might like to dodge this responsibility, as often as we hear about scams and deception by those posing to be in need when they really aren't, as little as we think we can spare from our own limited income—the fact remains that God takes the poor seriously. He is not obscure about this issue. He makes himself abundantly clear that he wants us to reach out to those in need, as a demonstration of his character.

I live in the somewhat unique city of Colorado Springs, now home to nearly a hundred ministry organizations. Many of them are small, but several employ hundreds of people and operate with nine-figure budgets. The Christian presence in this city is noticeable.

My pastor grew up in Colorado Springs, went away for a number of years, and was called back in late 1999 to lead his home church. He began his pulpit ministry a few weeks before his wife and sons could relocate from another city, so he was in town alone. One weekday he stopped at a fast-food restaurant for a quick lunch. Sitting at the table, he could not help overhearing a group of burly men talking nearby. Their shirts identified them as employees of a moving company.

"Yeah, this town has sure gone down the last few years," one man said. "It used to be a nice place to live, but now—"

"That's for sure," another chimed in. "It's horrible. Can't stand it around here anymore."

My pastor perked up his ears. What had gone wrong in this, the city of his birth? Had the drug trade run rampant? Was crime a lot worse now than he had assumed from earlier experience? Were the police overrun with corruption?

He kept listening. To his amazement, the moving crew eventually pinpointed what they felt was the source of all the trouble: the influx of new Christian organizations. The men proceeded to spell out various complaints about hypocrisy, hardheadedness on certain issues, and the like.

What?! How can this be? the native son asked himself. If men such as these were offended by the cross, that would be one thing. But their gripes had more to do with how God's people were conducting themselves. He sat mystified.

"And then, right there at that Wendy's table," he said when he told this story later to our congregation, "the Lord spoke to my heart as clearly as anything that has ever happened in my life. I truly believe it was a word for my future ministry at this church. All of a sudden I was overwhelmed with this sentence: *I want you to demonstrate my love in this city—with no strings attached.* That thought has kept ringing in my spirit ever since."

This has indeed become the watchword of our church in the succeeding years, worked out in a number of ways. From building Habitat for Humanity homes to producing a free July 4th festival in the park each summer, to hosting community events in our building free of charge, we are seeking to share God's love in the community. We're not the only church to move in this direction. Other congregations have adopted similar mindsets in recent times, helping to counteract those negative impressions.

The apostle Paul wrote to one church that had embarrassed itself in the public eye with several unfortunate incidents, "You yourselves are our letter . . . known and read by everyone. You show that you are a letter from Christ, the result of our ministry, written not with ink but with the Spirit of the living God, not on tablets of stone but on tablets of human hearts" (2 Cor. 3:2–3). He wanted this church to be known not for its infighting and its moral lapses but for modeling the life and love of Jesus.

The point gets across most directly and powerfully when love is focused on those in obvious need, those who cannot reciprocate, those who will never write large checks back to the church or polish its social standing. When the community "reads" that kind of "letter" in our actions, it is forced to assume the presence of genuine caring, not just self-serving ambition.

Why did India, a massive country with fewer than 4 percent Christians, pour out such lavish respect and condolence when Mother Teresa passed away in 1997? Her funeral drew the nation's highest leaders and was shown everywhere on live television. One Hindu speaker after another eulogized her memory. Religious dogma was laid aside for a day. Why?

The answer is obvious: she wholeheartedly served the poor and taught others to do the same. What she had done in the slums of Calcutta for a lifetime trumped all other opinions about her faith.

The gospel Jesus came to proclaim is undeniably "good news to the poor" (Luke 4:18). That's what he said when he stood up in his home synagogue to begin his public ministry. Let us never forget it. Any message or presentation of Christian faith that dodges this aspect is incomplete. It will never generate the full impact it was meant to carry.

How? Where? What Methods?

Fortunately, there is no shortage of channels for reaching out to the desperate. We cannot say we're willing but don't know how to proceed. The options are plentiful.

One option is to concentrate on *making a long-term difference in the life of just one individual.* Child sponsorship programs do this with excellence. For just twenty-five to thirty dollars a month, a boy or girl in an impoverished nation can be lifted out of hopelessness toward a productive adulthood. The money pays for school fees, adequate clothing, one nutritious meal a day, health screening, medicine as needed, and a loving introduction to the Savior in age-appropriate ways, all delivered by local people who genuinely care. Three organizations that do this well are Compassion International,[1] Mission of Mercy,[2] and World Vision[3]; no doubt there are others that could be named. The first two focus almost exclusively on raising up tomorrow's leaders from today's needy children; the third (World Vision) is a larger, more multifaceted organization that, like the Salvation Army, includes children as one of its emphases.

All of them have worked long enough among the poor to know that better roads and sewer systems and electric lines alone will not conquer poverty. Something must happen inside the hearts and minds of *people* to reverse centuries of despair and exploitation. That is why they concentrate on the most shapeable of the population, the young. And such work does not go unnoticed by government officials and business leaders, regardless of their politics.

In the more developed nations of the world, we still need to reach out to the underprivileged. One out of every six American children, for example, lives below the poverty line. For all of our elaborate government aid programs, we still have hunger and unnecessary sickness in the United States. A friend of mine who grew up in such conditions in central California started an outreach back in 1994 called Convoy of Hope.[4] It now delivers massive amounts of food and other supplies to needy American communities (some thirty sites each year) in a most interesting, highly visible format. On a given Saturday, loaded semitrucks roll up to a large parking lot near a struggling part of town so volunteers can start handing out free groceries. People come by the thousands to get food. On the same parking lot are information tables with employment options to consider, health screening booths, free haircuts, carnival rides for kids, plus chairs and an open-air stage so the gospel can be presented while people listen, wait in line, or stand on the edges. It turns into a festival atmosphere.

The result is that people go home with far more than a sack of groceries. They return to their homes with the knowledge that somebody cares about their struggle after all. They've been in touch with a God who sees their difficulty and has provided practical, hands-on assistance. Many enter a personal relationship with Christ as a result.

Every such event, obviously, requires at least a thousand volunteers to operate. In this way, Christian people put legs to their stated values. They reach out and touch hurting neighbors, even taking time to pray with them right there on the asphalt. Some recipients give their tattered lives to Christ that very day.

And of course, the news media show up. Convoy of Hope, with its colorful trucks and rides, is a great photo op. The cameras roll, and by the time the Saturday evening news has finished and the Sunday morning papers have been delivered, the entire city learns that Christians actually care about the poor.

While this kind of special event makes a certain impact, other more low-key ministries are built for ongoing service. Love INC (Love In the Name of Christ)[5] is one such structure that mobilizes the churches of a given city to find out about and serve local people with food, housing, and work needs. Its uniqueness is that it prevents duplication of effort; someone asking for help is first interviewed by a Love INC staff member, who determines what really needs to be done and then taps the church or agency in town best prepared to meet that need. The tendency of some individuals to go from one church to the next to the next seeking aid is thus prevented. The system is unified to provide what this person truly needs, without overlap.

Love INC now operates its clearinghouse model in 120 communities across 29 states and Puerto Rico. It has moved thousands of families off welfare, helped older citizens find safety and assistance in their living challenges, guided single teenage mothers toward stability, and responded to a wide array of other difficulties—with efficiency. Christians have thus been able to work together across traditional lines to maximize their impact for good.

But not everything has to be this centralized. Christians in small towns or with little resources can demonstrate one-way kindness as well, for the benefit of God's cause in the world. It usually starts with simply noticing a need and figuring out a commonsense response that evidences the spirit of Jesus. Allow me to give an illustration from my own local setting.

As a result of our pastor's emphasis on showing the love of Christ with no strings attached, we began to think about what might be done for nearby public schools. A woman in our congregation teaches at an elementary school in a less-affluent part of town. While you certainly wouldn't call it a slum, the fact is that households in that neighborhood are struggling; 56 percent of them are rentals (compared to 33 percent statewide). Three out of four children at this school qualify for free or subsidized lunches. A brave principal and her staff are trying their best to maintain educational effectiveness.

In such a climate, it's hard enough to provide what's needed for reading, writing, and arithmetic, let alone some of the ancillary subjects like music. The school owned only four band instruments, and few families could afford to rent their own; as a result, the band had only twelve players. Concerts were less than impressive.

Then one Sunday, our pastor stood up to say, "I'm just wondering . . . how many of us have an instrument sitting in a dark closet of our house somewhere gathering dust? What if you dug out that old trumpet, clarinet, or flute so we could bless Pikes Peak School with more instruments?" People began digging in their attics and storage units, and within a few weeks, more than a dozen usable instruments had been collected. A music store in town heard about the effort and volunteered to do free refurbishing.

Upon inspection, one of the saxophones turned out to be a professional grade Selmer instrument worth several thousands of dollars! Rather than hand this over to a novice fourth grader, it was decided to sell the sax for its real value and use the proceeds in more far-reaching ways. Came the day when a deacon of our church walked into the school to deliver fourteen different band instruments, all ready to play, plus a check for $4,300. He also brought news of church members with musical training who were willing to tutor young students after school.

The grateful music teacher used the money to buy ten more electronic keyboards for her music lab. Word spread throughout the community as well as the school district offices about what a church had done. The district website ran an article with photos entitled "Local Church Expands Music Opportunities at Pikes Peak" and gave glowing accolades. Heartfelt appreciation came back through the thank-you notes of kids, teachers, and parents alike. In addition to the free instruments now available, a ripple effect began, as more parents dug into their own pockets to rent an instrument for their son or daughter after all. At the next school concert, there were thirty players instead of twelve.

All because a congregation elected to focus on a local need and tried to make a difference.

An entire book could be filled with the ways God's people are demonstrating his love to the weak, the sick, the disenfranchised, the struggling. Christians all over the land are busy befriending immigrants . . . teaching English as a second language . . . driving the elderly to their appointments . . . giving single moms a break from their round-the-clock responsibility . . . visiting the prisons . . . fixing and serving meals in soup kitchens . . . counseling unwed mothers-to-be . . . providing foster care to children whose homes have disintegrated . . . relating to alienated teenagers . . . sheltering victims of hurricanes and fires . . . teaching financial management to those in serious debt. Each one of these has the potential to help the image of God's people in the world by showing that we are concerned about far more than church budgets and self-preservation. We are about the business of healing in a world of hurt.

Some would write off these kinds of things as simply "do-good" work. Yes, it is—and why not? Three different times on one page of the short book of Titus, we are exhorted to give ourselves to this kind of ministry (italics added):

> . . . Jesus Christ, who gave himself for us . . . to purify for himself a people that are his very own, *eager to do what is good.*
>
> 2:13–14

> Remind the people . . . to be obedient, to be *ready to do whatever is good.*
>
> 3:1

> I want you to stress these things, so that those who have trusted in God may be careful to *devote themselves to doing what is good.* These things are excellent and profitable for everyone.
>
> 3:8

The result, said Paul, is "that in every way [we] will make the teaching about God our Savior attractive" (2:10). Action enhances doctrine. Engaging real difficulties in a real world gives substance to the faith we profess.

Whether spoken or silent, the ministry of compassion says a mouthful.

12

Clearing the Fog

It was a muggy July evening in Atlanta, and the convention I was attending wrapped up its business by five-thirty. On the exhibit floor, I had met three friends from England the day before, and, trying to be a gracious host, I had said, "Maybe we could go do something together tomorrow night."

"Yes," one of them replied. "We read in the hotel flyer that the Atlanta Braves are playing. We're curious to see an American baseball game. Of course, we know cricket—but we don't understand how your game is played at all."

"Fine!" I said. "I'll accompany you to the game and be your 'tutor.'"

It turned out to be an intriguing experience. My explanations had to begin almost as soon as we left the parking lot. A fellow on the sidewalk wearing shorts and a green T-shirt had four tickets to sell for "just ten dollars apiece." I studied his tickets to see how good the seats were, made sure they were really for *tonight's* game instead of some other date, and finally said to my friends, "Yes, this is a good deal." We each pulled out money to acquire our tickets. As we walked away, the Brits had all kinds of questions about this peculiar process.

When we got inside, the players were out on the field warming up. Now my tutoring began in earnest. "Okay, the Braves are in the dark blue shirts with red numbers, while the Florida Marlins are in the white pinstripes. Florida is the state just south of here, by the way. Do you know what a 'brave' is? It means a young warrior in a Native American tribe. . . . Now, do you see the two long white lines stretching down each side of the field? They're made of chalk. Those are called the 'foul lines,' and the only hits that do any good have to occur between those two lines. . . . Each team uses nine players at a time. Of course, they have more players who can come into the game as substitutes—but once you leave the game, you're done for the night. In other words, it's like your 'football' and rugby. It's *not* like our basketball or hockey, where a player can come in and out and in again.

"Now let me explain the two kinds of pitches thrown. A good pitch is above home plate and between the batter's knees and mid-chest; that's called a strike. A bad pitch, outside that zone, is called a ball. Yes, I know the whole game is about 'ball,' but this is a particular use of the word. . . ."

On and on the explanations went; I felt like I was talking nonstop for hours. I had to explain "single" and "double" and "home run" and why a Marlin home run didn't cause much of a stir but a Braves home run sent the crowd crazy, with fireworks and screaming. When a base runner succeeded in stealing second base, my friends wondered why the square white bag was still out there in its place if the guy had "stolen" it. At one point a batter swung and broke his bat, the fat end soaring out toward the pitcher's head. That was an exciting moment to clarify.

Of course, as soon as the Turner Field fans began their trademark tomahawk chant, with thirty thousand right arms chopping downward as people groaned out the three-note minor-key melody over and over, I had to explain what in the world this was all about: what a tomahawk is in Native American culture, what you do with it, and how this ties into the Braves ethos at a baseball game.

My British friends were very attentive students. I didn't give them a test at the end, but they seemed to grasp a fair amount of what was going on. "Thank you for helping us understand!" they said. As we headed back to our rental car, I actually felt tired from so much mental effort, translating terms and actions so they could grasp them. For them, almost nothing was "obvious." It all needed enlightenment.

Without my running commentary, they would have understood very little of what they saw that night.

Jargon Jungle

Sports is, of course, not the only field in need of interpretation. Nearly every one of us has at some time tried to install, register, and actually learn to use a new piece of computer software. The buzz of language we don't understand has just about driven us crazy. *Why can't these very smart people talk in plain English?* we wonder.

Government has its share of word muck as well, like "ground-mounted confirmatory route markers" (those are road signs, in case you didn't get it). Did you know that homeless people are actually "urban campers"? A kid with a can of spray paint messing up a building with graffiti is a "wall artist."

If the wall artist showed up at school, he would not flunk tests; he would "achieve a deficiency." Students don't learn to write anymore; they "generate text" out of "writing elements," "tagmemic invention," "paradigmatic analysis," and "heuristics." When they get done, they can go to the "wellness activity center"—what you and I used to call the gym.

Speaking of wellness, my health insurer wants me to know that if I have two policies that seem as if they both might cover an expense,

> A Coverage Plan that does not contain a coordination of benefits provision that is consistent with this provision is always primary. There is one exception: coverage that is obtained by virtue of membership in a group that is designed to supplement a part of a basic package of benefits may provide that the supplementary coverage shall be excess to any other parts of the Coverage Plan provided by the contract holder. Examples of these types of situations are major medical coverages that are superimposed over base Coverage Plan hospital and surgical benefits, and insurance type coverages that are written in connection with a closed panel Coverage Plan to provide out-of-network benefits.

I think I feel better already.

Here is my point: the spiritual world can be just as dense, at least in the complex forms we have adopted over the years. Check any textbook of standard theology, or even your church's statement of faith, and see if nonbelievers could make sense of it. Noted Christian author Philip Yancey, whose books fight mightily (and successfully) to be understandable, says we are handicapped by being "children of the Reformation" (at least those of us Christians in the West). This makes us habitually conceptual, abstract, and theoretical. We naturally tend toward heavy, gray hypotheses that mean something to us but lack color and life.

I love this parody of Matthew 16:15–17.

> And Jesus said unto them, "Who do you say that I am?"
>
> And they answered, "You are the eschatological manifestation of the ground of being, the kerygma in which we find ultimate meaning of our interpersonal relationships, the totally Other in whom we subsist."
>
> And Jesus said, "WHAT??"

This kind of communication just will not get the job done for any ambassador of Christ. The simple, vital message is that God loved the world enough to send Jesus, who took the awful penalty for our sin, making us eligible to join God's family. We dare not encrust this message with fancy words and convoluted logic that suffocate the impact. If our job, like that of any diplomat, is to communicate effectively across cultural lines, we must pay close attention to our language.

Granted, the poorest preaching has sometimes brought men and women to Christ regardless. Stories could be told to make that point. The Holy Spirit's conviction has occasionally triumphed despite human garbling. But that is no excuse. Dr. Em Griffin, long-time professor of communication at Wheaton College, writes, "God can overrule our bumbling efforts, but it's irresponsible to expect him to do so if we haven't taken the trouble to discover the best possible means of persuasion."[1] We have to at least try to be clear.

This happens on at least three levels:

1. Choose Effective Vocabulary

If certain terms lead the hearer down a detour, it's our problem to solve. One student research project queried people in a shopping mall on what first came to mind when they heard the word *saved.* Most common answer: "What I wish I'd done with my last paycheck."[2] We'd probably get further talking about *being set free*—which is what Jesus himself did in John 8:32: "You will know the truth, and the truth will set you free."

Some in his audience, proud of their ethnic heritage, retorted:

> "We are Abraham's descendants and have never been slaves of anyone. How can you say that we shall be set free?"
>
> Jesus replied, "Very truly I tell you, everyone who sins is a slave to sin. Now a slave has no permanent place in the family, but a son belongs to it forever. So if the Son sets you free, you will be free indeed."
>
> vv. 33–36

Many people today would frankly admit that their lives are cramped by fears and worries, by compulsive behaviors, by abusive relationships. The idea of *freedom* or *liberation* sounds quite appealing. And that is exactly what Jesus came to bring. It is up to us to make sure that promise comes through loud and clear.

Another frequently used text to explain salvation is Romans 10:9. "If you confess with your mouth, 'Jesus is Lord,' and believe in your heart that God raised him from the dead, you will be saved" (NIV). The only trouble is that *confess* is an entirely negative word to modern hearers, as in "Okay, I confess I embezzled ten thousand dollars from the company." Or, "Yeah, I confess I ate all the ice cream." It means to admit, even though you'd rather not. So why would anyone want to admit reluctantly that Jesus is Lord? It doesn't make sense. The whole Christian definition of *confess* as a positive statement simply doesn't exist in the modern vocabulary.

Even most recent Bible translation teams have been tone-deaf to this problem. Finally, the TNIV (Today's New International Version) got it right for today's readers with this rendering: "If you declare with your mouth, 'Jesus is Lord' . . ."

We would do well to go through the same drill with such Christian words as "lost," "blessed," "repent," "born again," and "eternal life." Then we could get around to "justification" and "anointing" and "inerrancy." Our goal should not be to show off our erudite education but to connect with ordinary listeners. The more concise, the more memorable, the better.

Thomas Jefferson, whose way with words helped define the American Revolution, once said, "The most valuable of all talents is that of never using two words when one will do." And the words need to be short and clear, for maximum impact. If Prime Minister Winston Churchill (to choose another world-class statesman) had stood up in the House of Commons that fateful day of May 13, 1940, and said, "I have nothing to offer but casualties, exertion, disappointment, and perspiration," would the British people have rallied to his cause? Hardly.

Instead, he chose short, clipped, hard-hitting Anglo-Saxon words: "I have nothing to offer but blood, toil, tears, and sweat." His listeners clenched their teeth and vowed to pay the price of defeating the Nazi menace, whatever it took.

Words are more than "just words." They advance the great causes of humanity. And the cause of Christ is the greatest of all.

2. Use Effective Reasoning

The flow of our individual words must eventually add up to compelling points. The sum of the parts must turn out to be a convincing whole. They cannot be like the sarcastic sticker that once appeared in a Vancouver men's room on the air dryer beside the wash basins: "Press this button to hear a message from the Prime Minister."

How many sermons and teachings have you heard that were just like that—a rush of hot air that went on and on for a while but articulated almost nothing? How many articles and books? (Hopefully, not this one!) I remember my mother, then in her seventies, telling me about a guest speaker who had come to the Iowa church she and my father faithfully attended. "He read a Scripture text and then started into his message," she said, "and for a good twenty-five minutes I couldn't figure out for the life of me where he was going. His thoughts just didn't travel in a straight line. Then, *finally*, he turned a corner, and I got it! The point finally became clear at last."

That's nice . . . but most people are not as diligent as my mother to sit still for twenty-five minutes of fog. They need to catch the significance a lot faster than that—especially if they are not cooped up in a church pew from which it would be impolite to escape. The attention span of the modern listener and reader is getting shorter all the time, due to fast-paced media. We have to connect quickly, or not at all.

One thing that believers and skeptics alike will say about Jesus of Nazareth is this: he was never boring. "The crowds were amazed at his teaching, because he taught as one who had authority, and not as their teachers of the law" (Matt. 7:28–29). Actually, that seems almost backwards. The teachers of the law had the proper credentials, whereas Jesus had none. Yet who spoke *with authority*? The man who grew up in a carpenter's shop. Whenever he opened his mouth, people were riveted. Not that they always understood his stories—but they were intrigued nonetheless. They wanted to figure them out. His train of thought was vivid, compelling, and incisive.

After he left, his agents carried on in the same way. "When they [the religious establishment] saw the courage of Peter and John and realized that they were unschooled, ordinary men, they were astonished and they took note that these men had been with Jesus" (Acts 4:13). In other words, like Master, like follower. These dropout fishermen were packing the same wallop in their speech and actions as the now-departed Jesus.

Clearly, Jesus wants the same kind of representation today.

3. Tailor the Message to the Individual

Not every listener is the same, of course. And it is hard to read some people's sensitivities and prejudices in the first instant. It calls for all our powers of observation. Leighton Ford, the evangelist (and brother-in-law of Billy Graham), once said that in seeking to share the gospel, "you carefully feel around the rim of a person's soul until you come to a crack." I love that imagery. It conveys the idea of waiting, waiting, studying, listening, pausing . . . until something in the person's life goes, *Ah! Ouch—that's the spot where my hurt resides.*

A great illustration comes from John MacArthur, a well-known pastor and author from Southern California. When I heard the beginning of this story on a cassette, I was initially skeptical, because it happened on an airplane, and I had heard so many phony witnessing-on-airplanes stories in my life. But this one rang true.

MacArthur was flying to El Paso to speak at a men's conference, and after the plane took off, he got out his Bible and his notes to review his upcoming message. The man sitting next to him appeared, by complexion, to be from the Middle East.

After a while, the man said in a gentle accent, "Excuse me, sir, but I see you have a Bible. I am new to your country, and I don't understand your religion. In my country, everybody is Muslim. But here it is very confusing."

"Yes, I know," MacArthur replied.

"Maybe you could answer a question for me. Can you tell me the difference between a Catholic, a Protestant, and a Baptist?"

The pastor refrained from smiling as he proceeded to give a quick outline of the distinctions. He clarified that Baptists were part of the Protestant grouping, not something separate. He wound up saying that all the groups try to deal with human sin and the way to be right with God.

Then, instead of dropping the conversation and returning to his work, he wisely continued, "Now since you asked me a question, may I ask you one?"

"Yes, of course."

"Do Muslims have sins?" MacArthur already knew the answer, of course, but he wanted to see where the question would lead.

"Sins?!" the man exclaimed. "We have many, many sins! We have so many sins I don't even know them all!"

"Really?" said the pastor. "Well . . . do you do them?"

"Oh, all the time," the man freely admitted. "In fact, I am going to El Paso to do some sins! When I first immigrated into America, I came through here, and I met a girl. I'm going to see her. . . . We will sin this weekend!"

Again, MacArthur kept a straight face as he took the next step. "Well, um, how does God feel about your sins?"

The man turned somber. "It's bad," he replied. "Very bad."

"How bad is it?"

"It's so bad I could go to hell."

"But you're going to do it anyway?"

At this, the man replied with great feeling, "I *hope* . . . the God . . . will forgive me." He stared intently at the seat in front of him.

MacArthur waited a moment, and then continued, "Why do you think God would do that?"

"I don't know. I just hope that he will."

"On the basis of what?"

"I don't know. I just hope. . . ."

Then the pastor leaned forward to say slowly, in a quiet voice, "Well . . . I happen to know him personally . . . and I can tell you that he *won't* forgive you."

The man's head jerked up in shock, and his eyes grew wide—but not at the prospect of being unforgiven. What had shocked him was the first part of the sentence. "You know God personally?" It almost seemed as if he was thinking, *Then what are you doing here in the middle seat of the coach section on Southwest Airlines?!*

MacArthur replied, "I'm so sorry about the problem of your sin. Actually, I have some good news for you. We all have the same problem you mentioned. And that is why Jesus Christ came to this earth, to win the possibility of forgiveness for all our sins. . . ." From that point onward, the Good News unfolded.[3]

What a wonderful, creative, sensitive choice of words to bring the gospel to a person who was, underneath, anxious about his eternal destiny. The chance for reconciliation with a holy God was extended with both grace and clarity.

With a different type of person, however, such an approach would have failed. If a person held a cavalier attitude toward sin, denying its importance, then what? The message would need to be tailored another way.

Sarah E. Hinlicky, in a brilliant essay entitled "Talking to Generation X," painted just such a picture. Though she is a committed Christian, she eloquently described the worldview of her peers:

> We've never been proud to be Americans—our political memory stretches back only as far as Vietnam, Watergate, and Reaganomics. Our parents left religion and, perhaps not coincidentally, each other in unprecedented numbers. Failed ideologies were mother's milk to us: love didn't save the world, the Age of Aquarius brought no peace, sexual liberation brought us AIDS and legions of fatherless children, Marxism collapsed. We can't even imagine a world of cultural or national unity; our world is more like a tattered patchwork quilt. . . .
>
> We know you've tried to get us to church. That's part of the problem. Many of your appeals have been carefully calculated for success, and that turns our collective stomach. Take worship, for instance. You may think that fashionably cutting-edge liturgies relate to us on our level, but the fact is, we can find better entertainment elsewhere. The same goes for anything else you term "contemporary." We see right through it; it's up-to-date for the sake of being up-to-date, and we're not impressed by the results.

She then gets to the matter of "Absolute Truth"—a major component of the gospel.

> Gen Xers doubt the very existence of such Truth with a capital T. We're much more comfortable with the idea of a multiplicity of little truths than one single unifying truth. But

even if universal truth *does* exist, we are extremely skeptical that you—or anyone else—can possess it. . . .

It often sounds to us like the Church preaches two Gods, one of law and another of love. The first punishes sin (though we see evildoers get away with murder) while the second babysits his flock (but there's too much suffering for us to buy that, either). We refuse God's judgments, yet judge our parents harshly by canons in which hypocrisy is the only capital crime.

How in the world does any ambassador of Christ communicate with this generation? It feels as if all the doors are shut, the barriers stacked high. Disillusionment and cynicism have soured everything.

Not entirely, says Sarah Hinlicky. She eventually finds a crack of daylight:

What do you have left to persuade us? One thing: the story. We are story people. We know narratives, not ideas. Our surrogate parents were the TV and the VCR, and we can spew out entertainment trivia at the drop of a hat. We treat our ennui with stories, more and more stories, because they're the only things that make sense. . . . That's to your advantage: you have the best redemption story on the market.

Perhaps the only thing you can do, then, is to point us towards Golgotha, a story we can make sense of. Show us the women who wept and loved the Lord but couldn't change his fate. Remind us that Peter, the rock of the Church, denied the Messiah three times. . . . We recognize this world: ripped from the start by our parents' divorces, spoiled by our own bad choices, threatened by war and poverty, pain and meaninglessness. . . . We know all too well that we, too, would betray the only one who could save us.

One more thing. In our world where the stakes are high, remind us that all hope is not lost. As Christians you worship not at the time of the crucifixion, but Sunday morning at the resurrection. Tell us that the lives we lead now are redeemed. . . . We know that death will continue to break our hearts and our bodies, but it's not the end of the story.[4]

It is more than just sloganeering to say that Jesus's life, death, and life again constitutes The Greatest Story Ever Told. In ways more profound than any of us know, it speaks to the lives, fears, and deepest needs of postmoderns in the twenty-first century. It is perhaps the one "silver bullet" that penetrates the hardest human armor.

Whether through live drama at Christmas or Easter, through film, through sermons, or through a simple medium such as a child's picture book, the Story is at the core of God's message to a hurting world. No matter how familiar the ambassador finds it to be, it must be retold and retold to succeeding generations. It carries a power of unparalleled magnitude.

Whatever the time and place, whoever the listener, viewer, or reader, we are commissioned to get the message across. There's an old proverb among newspaper editors that says, "You can't flunk the reader." If the person on the other end of the process misunderstands the story, the article, the editorial . . . it is pointless to say they were not paying full attention, got derailed by their own biases, or some other excuse. It does no good to whine, "Well, I told it correctly; they just didn't get it." The professional communicator takes responsibility for framing the words and images in such a way that audiences and readerships get it straight, without distortion. That burden just goes with the territory.

Our prayer should parallel that of the apostle Paul, who wrote from a Roman dungeon, "Pray also for me, that whenever I speak, words may be given me so that I will fearlessly make known the mystery of the gospel, for which I am an ambassador in chains. Pray that I may declare it fearlessly, as I should" (Eph. 6:19–20). Those of us who live and work as God's envoys *outside* of prison walls should aspire to no less.

13

More Than Words

The most obtuse, convoluted, stuffy, long-winded class in my entire graduate-school program was "Communication Theory." I thought I'd never live through that swamp of abstract suppositions and murky research studies. At the end of the semester (I actually passed!), I would have gladly sold my 626-page black-covered textbook with its fifty-five essays by intellectuals far and wide. But I decided to hang on to it as a memorial to my perseverance. I still have it today.

One small bit of useful perspective I gleaned in that otherwise torturous class was that communication is more than verbal. It is words plus. We gather information via language but also via image and inflection and inference and demonstration. What people *say* (or write) is only part of the package.

So it is with the gospel. To articulate the Good News, and to do it well, is extremely important. We spent the entire previous chapter talking about this. But there's an additional dimension to consider in the process. It is the role of divine power to touch human lives.

The original messengers whom Jesus deployed as he left this earth "went out and preached everywhere, *and the Lord worked with them* and confirmed his word by the signs that accompanied it" (Mark 16:20, italics added). They talked—but that wasn't all. God stepped up alongside them and reinforced what they had said through visible demonstration.

Hebrews 2:3–4 says exactly the same thing: "This salvation, which was first announced by the Lord, was confirmed to us by those who heard him. *God also testified to it* by signs, wonders and various miracles, and by gifts of the Holy Spirit distributed according to his will" (italics added).

Logic plus exhibition. Verbiage plus voltage. Message plus manifestation. God is the Master Communicator, and he sends his emissaries out into the world with a multimedia approach. He wants us to speak and also display—in other words, to both "show and tell."

Says British author David Pawson in his book *Word and Spirit Together*, "We are to communicate the gospel by demonstration as well as declaration. People need to see as well as hear. This requires more than sound doctrine. An understanding of the person of the Spirit must be matched by an anointing with his power. We may deliver an excellent lecture *about* him but that may not develop an experienced life *in* him."[1]

It is not hard to see this happening in the New Testament. Consider the ministry of Paul, perhaps the most intellectual of the apostles. He certainly had no difficulty speaking with clarity and eloquence. He was an excellent communicator.

Yet listen to this account of his work in Iconium: "Paul and Barnabas spent considerable time there, speaking boldly for the Lord, who confirmed the message of his grace by enabling them to perform signs and wonders" (Acts 14:3). A few verses later, they moved down the road to neighboring Lystra, where "as he was speaking, Paul looked directly at [a paraplegic man], saw that he had faith to be healed and called out, 'Stand up on your feet!' At that, the man jumped up and began to walk" (Acts 14:9–10). The crowd went crazy at this point, assuming that the Roman pantheon of gods had shown up. Paul quickly explained the power of his God, and he had everyone's full attention.

We see no such demonstration a few chapters later when Paul entered the Athens "think tank" on Mars Hill (Acts 17). Granted, he gave a masterful presentation. He was culturally sensitive. He showed unique creativity in starting his remarks by alluding to a local shrine dedicated "TO AN UNKNOWN GOD" (v. 23). He deftly drew a link to the Lord Almighty. Soon he was quoting a well-known Stoic philosopher to bolster his arguments. It was an impressive piece of oratory.

Many Christian writers have held up this tour de force as an example of excellent evangelism. Indeed, Paul did far better that day than you or I would have done. He was brilliant.

Yet, what was achieved in the end? The closing paragraph of Acts 17 records that audience reaction was mixed. Some listeners scoffed, others were politely noncommittal ("We want to hear you again on this subject"), and a modest number believed the gospel (v. 32). Curiously, we don't know if an actual church ever got off the ground in Athens. If it did, the rest of Acts and the Epistles are entirely silent about it.

Paul's next stop in Acts 18 was Corinth, only fifty miles to the west. His efforts here resulted in one of the major congregations of the New Testament era. Was there something different about his ministry in this new place? Listen carefully to how he describes those early days:

When I came to you, I did not come with eloquence or human wisdom as I proclaimed to you the testimony about God. For I resolved to know nothing while I was with you except Jesus Christ and him crucified. I came to you in weakness with great fear and trembling. My message and my preaching were not with wise and persuasive words, but with a demonstration of the Spirit's power, so that your faith might not rest on human wisdom, but on God's power.

1 Corinthians 2:1–5

Reading between the lines, we see a man sobered and humbled. He sounds unsure that the Athens speech was that terrific after all. It's time to get back to basics, he tells himself. Just stick to Christ and the cross, backed up by nonverbal evidence of divine power. Paul, the man of letters and scholarship, seems chastened not to get too fancy for his own good, or that of the cause.

During his months in Corinth, he wrote a letter to the church at Thessalonica, where he had been able to spend only three weeks in ministry before being run out of the city (see Acts 17:1–10). He remembered which approach had worked so well and so quickly in that place. "Our gospel came to you not simply with words but also with power, with the Holy Spirit and deep conviction" (1 Thess. 1:5). A few years later, he used similar language to summarize his career to that point:

I will not venture to speak of anything except what Christ has accomplished through me in leading the Gentiles to obey God by what I have said and done—by the power of signs and wonders, through the power of the Spirit of God. So from Jerusalem all the way around to Illyricum [modern Bosnia!], I have fully proclaimed the gospel of Christ.

Romans 15:18–19

Yes, But How?

While such scriptural evidence is inspiring, modern readers may pause wistfully to wonder if such a double strategy is
still feasible today. Can we in the twenty-first century hope
to present God's truth in both words and powerful demonstration? Isn't the second half of that equation up to God
alone, who doesn't seem nearly as energetic these days as
he was back then?

The answer to this has several parts. Yes, we freely admit
that we cannot force God to do miracles on demand. We
cannot snap our fingers at dramatic moments to heal the
sick or deliver the oppressed. He alone holds that kind of
power.

But if we never ask, we will not receive. If we do not seek,
we shall never find. When our mental paradigm omits the
supernatural, it is not likely to force its way in. If we have
convinced ourselves that signs and wonders were peculiar
to the apostolic era (the first century), then God will most
often let us labor under that constraint.

Certain theologies have endeavored to draw this kind
of line. But the evidence throughout church history and
the testimony of godly leaders takes a more open view. To
cite just one: John Wesley wrote to Thomas Church in June
1746 as follows:

> I do not know that God hath anyway precluded himself from
> thus exerting his sovereign power, from working miracles
> in any kind or degree, in any age, to the end of the world.
> I do not recollect any scripture wherein we are taught, that
> miracles were to be confined within the limits either of the
> apostolic or the Cyprianic [third century] age; or of any
> period of time, longer or shorter, even till the restitution
> of all things.[2]

If we in the West wish to regain a sense of the full-orbed gospel, we would do well to look to what is happening in other parts of the world. The accounts of Muslims in various lands turning to Christ after seeing him in a dream are now too numerous to be discounted. God is demonstrating his reality in the most unlikely places.

David Howard, former international director of the World Evangelical Fellowship, verified the following example that took place in a restricted country before the fall of communism. He got it from a pastor whose young son in second grade had to endure the daily taunts of an aggressively Marxist teacher. One day she said sneeringly to the class, "Some people say there is a God up in heaven who will give you what you ask for. Let's test that out and see if he does. We need more books, workbooks, paper, and pencils in this school. Let's ask God to give them to us."

She then proceeded to voice a mock "prayer."

A few minutes later, when nothing had happened, she smiled and said, "See, children? There is no God up in heaven. He didn't hear us, and he didn't send anything."

The pastor's son and others from Christian homes squirmed silently in their seats, embarrassed. But that afternoon, just as school was letting out for the day, they exited the building to find a large truck arriving with a fresh load of educational supplies. They watched in amazement as the driver opened the back doors and began hauling the books, workbooks, paper, and pencils inside.

"Teacher! Teacher! Come quickly!" the children shouted. "Here are the things you asked God to send! See? He sent them!" An entire classroom of children plus one very baffled teacher had been confronted with the power of a listening God.

Closer to Home

Would God ever do such a thing in North America or Western Europe? Certainly. He is not biased toward frontier situations. He is eager to bring people of every nationality closer to his reality.

Rich Nathan, the Columbus, Ohio, pastor I quoted in chapter 6, tells about talking with a server at his favorite Starbucks coffee shop one day, who said she had terrible insomnia. She claimed she hadn't slept in months. Rich offered a few words of sympathy and then went back to his table to continue his work while sipping his cappuccino. The Holy Spirit seemed to nudge him, however, to ask the young woman if he might pray about her problem. The conversation went like this, he recalls:

"You mentioned that you can't sleep and that you haven't slept for months. I'm a Christian pastor over at the Vineyard near here. Would you mind if I prayed for you that you might be able to get a good night's sleep?"

She said, "Vineyard? Man, all of your people come in here. I've watched you guys grow. You must be doing a great thing. But I haven't been in church for years."

I said, "I don't think that really matters now. Would it be OK if I prayed for you to be able to get to sleep?"

She said, "That'd be fine. It's very nice of you to offer to pray for me."

I said, "No, I mean right now. Would it be OK if I prayed for you right now, right here?"

She flushed a little bit and said, "Well, I guess so."

I said, "Well, you'll need to come out from behind the counter so I can pray for you."

Hesitating, she walked out from behind the counter and said, "You know I haven't been in church for years."

I said, "I know. You said that before. But it really doesn't matter to God. I'm still able to pray for you." I asked her right there in the center of Starbucks if it would be OK if I put my hand on her while we prayed.

She said, "That would be fine."

I prayed very simply that God, who loves her, would come and heal her body, calm her mind, and allow her to sleep.

A week later I walked into Starbucks. Her entire countenance had changed. She ran out from behind the counter and said, "Rich, I've been looking for you. Let me give you a hug." She threw her arms around me and said, "I've been healed. I've never felt better in my life. The night after you prayed for me I had the best night's sleep I'd had in months. I feel like a totally new person. I can't tell you how good I feel. Thank you."

I said, "You know it wasn't me who healed you. It was God."

She said, "Yeah, I think I believe that. I think it was God."

I then asked her if she would come to church. She laughed and said, "You know I told you I hadn't been in church for years. But here's the deal. I promise you that in the next couple of weeks I'm going to come to church."

What that server from Starbucks needed is what many postmodernists need. They don't need a clever argument or a canned evangelistic approach. They need a touch from God.[3]

Giant strides such as this are feasible when the Good News of words-plus-power is brought to bear on human need. The person's mind, body, and spirit are all engaged. As I said earlier, it's a multimedia approach, which develops more impact than any single medium can muster. The God who speaks becomes also the God who touches us in the deepest part of our being.

Even Jesus, the Son of God, uses this combination tactic. One of his most well-known discussions with a nonbeliever (again, studied and dissected in numerous lectures on evangelism) was with the Samaritan woman at the well. He strikes up a casual conversation with her about water. Then the dialogue basically goes nowhere for eleven verses (John 4:7–17). He says something about "living water," and she clearly doesn't get it. She wants a plumbing solution in her house so she doesn't have to make this daily trek out to the well. It almost seems the two of them are talking past each other, not making any connection.

Then—Jesus unleashes one sentence that is clearly supernatural. It is what 1 Corinthians 12, in its list of spiritual gifts, calls "a message of knowledge" (v. 8). Jesus suddenly comes out with some classified information: the woman has been through five marriages and is now living with guy number six. *Whoa!* This stops her cold.

From that instant, she is paying full attention. She wants to hear every word this stranger says. She must comprehend the source of his power. By the end of the day, not only has she become God's forgiven daughter, but "many of the Samaritans from that town believed in him because of the woman's testimony, 'He told me everything I ever did'" (John 4:39). The impact of the divine revelation by the well reverberated through the entire community. Their daily routine had been jostled. People had to find out what this was all about.

God is still in the business of disrupting human rhythms and confronting them with his greater self. As long as people are comfortable and half-asleep, they can tune out the message from heaven. But when their lives are interrupted by something clearly divine, they start paying attention.

Healing for Whom?

In fact, the whole ministry of healing in the apostolic era is far more slanted toward evangelistic purposes than many of us realize. When we ourselves or our loved ones are in pain or discomfort, we want God to heal *us*. We pray fervently, "O God, have mercy on your servant. Come and touch with your mighty power." After all, we have been his child for many years now, and we feel we have a right to call for his intervention.

All that is true. The familiar passage in James 5 invites us to receive the elders' anointing with oil for our healing. This is quite within the New Testament scope of benefits for those who love the Lord.

However . . . what about the larger picture? I did a personal study once of all the recorded occasions when a healing occurred in the book of Acts and the Epistles, taking special note of *who* was healed—believer or unbeliever. The results caught me by surprise. Out of sixteen distinct incidents, only four brought healing to believers! The other twelve (75 percent) were unbelievers such as the beggar at the Beautiful Gate (Acts 3), the Philippi slave girl (Acts 16), and the father of Publius on the island of Malta (Acts 28). In each of the dozen cases, there was an immediate and dramatic breakthrough for the gospel.

Yes, again I acknowledge the four cases with believers (Dorcas raised from the dead in Acts 9; Eutychus, who fell out of the window in Acts 20; Paul himself after snakebite in Acts 28; and his associate Epaphroditus in Philippians 2). Nevertheless, the weight of the historical record leans the other way, toward those who have not yet entered the family of God.

Wanted: A Serious Encounter

Whatever the merits of this particular analysis, the overall point is that our service as representatives of the King of kings is enhanced by showing him in all his splendor—verbal and nonverbal. He is truly unique. He roams outside all boxes and preconceptions. He is the world's Master.

And how convenient that the current culture seems to be yearning more than ever for the supernatural. Think about how many popular books, television shows, and films dabble in the paranormal. Interest in angels is at an all-time high. People are hungry to go beyond that which can be easily explained, it seems. Mystery is actually welcomed.

Leith Anderson is a respected Baptist pastor in suburban Minneapolis, author of such books as *A Church for the 21st Century,* and former interim president of the National Association of Evangelicals. With an eye practiced at studying the culture, he writes: "People tell me they are looking for a church where they can meet God, where there is the power of the Holy Spirit, and where their lives can be radically changed. We have a generation that is less interested in cerebral arguments, linear thinking, theological systems, and more interested in encountering the supernatural."[4]

If we feel inadequate to champion such power . . . if we feel like cowering in the shadows of the wonder-working apostles from long ago . . . if we are not sure about this part of an ambassador's work . . . we should take note of the example of Elisha in the Old Testament. A man of modest abilities (a simple farmer when God called him; see 1 Kings 19:19), he was hardly a star. He watched from the sidelines as his colorful mentor, Elijah, performed mighty miracles. But the day came when Elijah was swept up to heaven in a chariot of fire, and no one remained to speak for God except the mild-mannered Elisha.

In that moment, a spark ignited within him. He picked up the fallen cloak of the ascended prophet, walked back to the Jordan, suddenly slapped the water, and blurted out perhaps the boldest question of his life thus far: "Where now is the LORD, the God of Elijah?" (2 Kings 2:14). His words seem to imply a tone of expectation: *All right! It's time for action. Let the God of miracles show himself—now!*

The Jordan River split in two at that moment, and the public ministry of Elisha was launched. Bible scholars have pointed out that as the chapters of 2 Kings move along, twice as many Elisha miracles are recorded as Elijah ones were in 1 Kings. An entire nation was turned, at least for a season, to the worship of almighty God. Who would ever have dreamed it?

The God of Elijah, of Elisha, of Daniel, of the apostles is unchanging over the centuries. He still means to impress this world with his omnipotent power. It is part of his overall communication package. And he extends it to a waiting populace through us.

14

Damage Control

Sometimes the best intent goes awry. The most careful choice of words, the most fervent prayer, the most compassionate outreach, and the most dynamic miracle are still subject to the sabotage of misguided churchgoers who aren't thinking about the overall mission. As much as we seek to lift high the name of Christ in ways that today's world will understand and even desire, our "compatriots" can quickly undermine it all.

This makes us understandably frustrated, embarrassed, and even a touch angry. We mutter unkind things about people's lack of intelligence or sensitivity. We fear for the contempt that will surely arise in the minds of those outside our faith.

It's a little like how David K. E. Bruce, the American ambassador profiled in chapter 2, felt not long after taking his first post in the Paris embassy. He was quickly informed that

July 4th each year was to be an all-out party for American citizens in the area. He anticipated a rollicking good time in celebration of U.S. independence . . . but nothing like what actually transpired. The American notion of "liberty" took on a whole new meaning that holiday. His biographer writes:

> According to custom, anyone with an American passport had a right to attend. Bruce's first Glorious Fourth . . . gave him a rude shock. Eight thousand guests made short work of the wine-Cointreau-cognac punch. . . . The Bruces left in the early evening after the official reception, but the party continued and became increasingly rowdy. Marine guards summoned by the overwhelmed French gendarmes failed to restore order. Recalling the shambles years later, Bruce wrote, "Copulating couples refused to be dislodged from the shrubbery; incontinent individuals urinated and defecated on the front steps and the lawn."
>
> Although he made sure the party in following years was respectably sedate, he loathed it, and not just because he personally paid the caterer's bill. He tried unsuccessfully to persuade ambassadors to cancel the party throughout Europe. "There have been a good many complaints from individual American citizens," he argued, "that it is in bad taste, especially at the present time, to engage so publicly in what the natives of various countries sometimes regard as ostentation."[1]

We can well imagine Ambassador Bruce trying to apologize the next day to the French police for the behavior of his countrymen. We know the feeling, don't we? More than a few times in our lives we have had to say, "I'm truly sorry for what such-and-such a Christian said, or did. It was in poor taste and uncalled-for. Please don't define all of us by this unpleasant sampling."

Sometimes the offense has been shocking, as when those of pro-life conviction have opted to fire weapons at abortion clinics and their staff members. In some tragic cases, the cause of life ended up causing the opposite. Other times the attack has been not with bullets but with bombastic words, antagonizing everyone who hears or reads them.

More often, the provocation is simply a matter of tastelessness or even silliness. For some people, the quest to be clever or humorous overrides the good sense to remember how such words truly sound to an outsider.

What Next?

The challenge for spiritual envoys in these situations is to sort out how they personally feel at the moment versus what would be best for the cause of Christ. Our inner emotions no doubt want to spout off, to brand the offender as an idiot, to order him or her to keep quiet from this point on. Almost as quickly, however, something needs to be said to the watching society to mitigate the affront.

Damage control thus faces two directions. Helping outsiders understand what happened and why is an important task. Guiding insiders not to do it again is necessary as well.

In the first instance, it doesn't help to deny that the offense occurred, or to pretend it was insignificant. Far better to show clear-eyed realism and put the matter into a larger perspective. Dr. Peter Kuzmic, a Christian scholar from Slovenia who has spent a great deal of time studying and teaching in the United States (now at Gordon-Conwell Theological Seminary outside Boston), tells of being questioned by a reporter during one of the televangelist scandals. Kuzmic forthrightly gave this summary: "Charisma without character is catastrophe." He wasn't

161

being nasty; he was simply acknowledging the truth that public figures' native abilities and appeal are not enough. Without a bedrock of ethics, these people are at risk of being seduced by their own power and defrauding those who rely on them.

Such candor wins the respect of observers, both within the media and without.

Granted, it is a fine line to know how much to say. Some Christians err on the side of clamming up, admitting nothing at all, even if the facts are undeniable. This leaves a vacuum that some antagonists are more than happy to fill. Other Christians are too quick to join in the censure, condemning the miscreants in harsh language. They cannot seem to find words that distinguish without denigrating.

Most nonbelievers are astute enough, however, to know that no movement is perfect, and not all adherents are going to do the right thing 100 percent of the time. If we speak honestly about our shortcomings, even apologizing where it is warranted, the response can be healthy.

A friend of mine, Jon Lawson, is our church's worship and arts pastor. One Palm Sunday afternoon, he was working in his office getting ready for an evening choir rehearsal, when there was a tap on the window. He looked up to see the face of a young man in his early twenties. He didn't know him, but he could tell by his clothing—the white shirt with a tie, black pants, and an apron around his waist—that he worked as a restaurant waiter.

Jon motioned for him to come in and sit down.

The young man's expression was downcast. "Are you one of the preachers here?" he asked in a soft-spoken voice.

"Well, not exactly," Jon replied. "But I'm on the ministerial staff. How can I help you?"

"Well, I just need to tell someone. . . ." His face flushed a bit, and then he continued, "I work at a restaurant—I'm not gonna tell you which one—but I'd like for you to teach the congregation to show respect for those who serve them."

Jon answered, "Yes, we believe that very much. I've heard our senior pastor make that very point more than once from the pulpit. He's even said with a smile, 'If you're not going to tip appropriately, then you need to stay out of restaurants!'"

The young man looked up as if startled. "You're kidding!"

Jon paused a moment and then went on. "It sounds to me like something happened at work today. Want to tell me about it?"

The waiter began the story of a table full of Christians he had served. They talked openly about Christian things, even identifying the name of their church. But "they were the most rude customers I've ever waited on," he said. They were very demanding; they wanted everything *right now.* "Whatever I did was wrong—one thing after another. You wouldn't believe how I got yelled at.

"Finally, it was over. This turned out to be a fifty-eight-dollar tab—and they left a three-dollar tip.

"I earn $2.35 an hour. The rest of my money is all supposed to be tips. I almost quit my job just now. . . ."

Jon hung his head as he replied, "I am so sorry. That's awful! Nobody deserves to be treated that horribly."

The waiter continued. "After I got off my shift, I drove around for a while looking for their church but couldn't find it. So I stopped in here instead. I hope you don't mind."

"No, that's entirely fine. I'm actually glad you came in. People just lose their view sometimes that everyone is created in God's image. Everyone is important to God. The lousy thing is that even church people forget that. I've done it myself on occasion, I admit."

"Yeah, me too," the young man said, now breathing a little easier. "It's okay—you don't have to apologize. You weren't the one to give me a hassle."

"Well, yes, but we're all linked in a way. We all bear the name of 'Christian.' And that's why I think it's good for me to say I'm sorry." Jon fished into his pocket for some cash. Pulling it out, he said, "Here's the rest of your tip."

"No, no—you don't need to do that," the waiter protested, pushing his hand away.

"I really wish you'd take it," Jon replied.

"But it wasn't your fault."

"True. But this is Passion Week, you know? It's the time of year when we think about the fact that Jesus paid for all our sins and mistakes. He didn't have to do that—but he did."

The waiter eventually said he would accept the money and give it to some homeless person. Jon offered to pray with him. No, that wouldn't be necessary, the waiter said, but thanks anyway. The conversation ended some twenty minutes after it had started, with Jon saying, "Hey, if you ever have another hard day, feel free to stop by again so we can talk, okay?" Then the young man left, calmer and more reflective than he had entered.

How many people in all our lives are among the "walking wounded," having been belittled and even insulted by those who bear the badge of Christianity? They seldom say so as openly as this waiter, giving us a chance to make amends. But whenever we pick up a signal, however faint, that such injury has occurred, it is part of our duty to heal it as sensitively as we can.

Eyes on the Prize

The ministry of damage control requires being attuned, as we have said before, to the outside viewpoint, to the way our words and deeds come across to those who do not share our faith. It means stepping outside of our own skin to take on the perspectives of others. *What are they seeing and hearing? How is all this impacting them?*

It is interesting to watch the way the apostle Paul talked to Roman officials in his day about his intermittent conflicts with Jewish orthodoxy. As far as the idol-worshiping Romans were concerned, Jews and followers of "The Way" were fairly similar. They were both monotheistic, and both of them held passionately to their doctrines. When the temple mob surrounded Paul in Acts 21 and threatened to lynch him on the spot, the Romans had to intervene to restore civil order, no doubt rolling their eyes as to why these people couldn't just get along.

Two years later, Paul was still being bounced around the legal system and finally got a hearing before King Agrippa. Acts 26 gives a lengthy transcript of his court speech. It is notable what he did *not* say on that occasion. He could have waxed eloquent on how extremist and unreasonable the Jewish complainants were: "Your Majesty, these people are crazy. Their facts are contorted, and they are simply pursuing a vicious vendetta against me. . . ."

Paul did nothing of the kind. He treated his opponents with courtesy; in fact, he didn't talk much about them at all.

He could have instead zeroed in on the lack of due process in this case: "Your Majesty, my civil rights have been trampled in this matter. A great period of my life has been wasted sitting in prison waiting, waiting, waiting. Whatever happened to the guarantee of a fair and speedy trial? This is outrageous treatment of an innocent man who, may I remind the Court, holds the coveted treasure of Roman citizenship. . . ."

Paul did not go this route either.

Instead, he viewed this legal proceeding through an ambassador's eyes. How could he use this moment to bring the king closer to the reality of Christ? Paul opted to tell his personal life story. He began with his upbringing as a Pharisee, told about his early persecution of "The Way," then described his dramatic conversion, highlighted his call to ministry . . . and before anyone quite knew where he was headed, he was appealing for the monarch's soul. "King Agrippa, do you believe the prophets? I know you do" (v. 27).

The king was thrown off-guard. He asked defensively, "Do you think that in such a short time you can persuade me to be a Christian?" (v. 28).

Paul confidently responded, "Short time or long—I pray God that not only you but all who are listening to me today may become what I am, except for these chains" (v. 29).

That is what we might call a masterful reframing of the debate. His quarrel with the Jewish leaders was left far behind in the dust. He deftly brought the discussion to eternal matters. More than arguing for his personal freedom, he was representing a Savior who reached out in love to every person in the courtroom that day.

Shortsighted outbursts and *ad hominem* retaliations do not help in the wake of an embarrassing event that has smudged Jesus's reputation. The wise, self-controlled diplomat goes instead about the business of mopping up, limiting the damage as much as possible, and seeking to find perhaps even a fresh opening for the true gospel. This is all part of the job of being an envoy of heaven.

Epilogue

Giving Our Best

We work for the best, most credible cause in the world. Better than any political party or candidate . . . better than any social improvement crusade . . . better than any high-flying, profit-making corporation with a boatload of employee benefits—we enjoy the high honor and distinction of serving the King of kings. His agenda outshines all the rest. His goals are the answer to society's stresses.

As his ambassadors, we do not travel in long black limousines, live in a chateau surrounded by servants, or send our children to aristocratic schools. The trappings are not as elegant as those enjoyed by members of the diplomatic corps. But the work is supremely rewarding. This is a flag worth lifting high. This is an effort that will make a stunning difference in the world.

Others may complain about the cruelty and injustice of our times, the immorality of Western culture, the drudgery of daily existence. Christ stands in contrast to all that, offering not just "the good life" but what he called "life . . . to the full" (John 10:10). Actually, to be more precise, he offers it *through us*. We are his extension agents.

In the powerful words of E. Stanley Jones:

> The early Christians did not say in dismay: "Look what the world has come to," but in delight, "Look what has come to the world." They saw not merely the ruin, but the Resources for the reconstruction of that ruin. They saw not merely that sin did abound, but that grace did much more abound. On that assurance the pivot of history swung from blank despair, loss of moral nerve, and fatalism, to faith and confidence that at last sin had met its match.[1]

This kind of mission is so vital that it deserves our very best shot. No halfhearted measures. No bonehead plays. No thoughtless gaffes in what we say when speaking for the Almighty. The kingdom of God merits the most excellent representation we can offer. We want to make heaven proud.

I was driving once on a lonely stretch of highway across the Texas Panhandle. While slowing down for a small town I noticed a motel that had no doubt been a modest place to start with—and by now, after several decades in the wind and heat of the High Plains, was showing its age all the more. What caught my eye was the name of the establishment: the "It'll Do Motel."

I smiled. The message of the name was that if you really needed a bed for the night and didn't require much more than that, well . . . it'll do.

Our service as God's delegates must rise to a higher standard than that. He wants quality. He wants thoughtful, intelligent representation in the world. He wants our full attention to the task at hand. This is not a burden for us; it is in fact the way we complete our purpose in life. Jesus said, "Seek first his kingdom and his righteousness, and all these things will be given to you as well" (Matt. 6:33). As we make God's priorities our own, concentrating on what he considers important, we look behind us and find that our personal needs have somehow been taken care of as well. We didn't even notice. He didn't drain the health and energy out of us in order to accomplish his goals. He has, in fact, enriched our lives simultaneously with extending his rule across the world.

When we live and work conscientiously for the sake of the cause, the result is a double blessing.

Notes

Chapter 1: Who, Us?

1. Frederick Buechner, *A Room Called Remember* (New York: HarperCollins, 1984), 142.

2. Mona Charen, "Minority of U.S. Soldiers Endanger America's Effort in Iraq" (Creator's Syndicate, May 8, 2004).

Chapter 2: Ambassadors at Work

1. Nelson D. Lankford, *The Last American Aristocrat* (Boston: Little, Brown, 1996), 216.

2. Ibid., 218.

3. Ibid., 328.

Chapter 3: The Christian "Brand"

1. *Business Week* double issue dated August 9–16, 2004.

2. Andrew Murray, "Turning Your Organization into a Powerful Brand" (BrandWorks Consulting seminar).

3. Robert Burns, "To a Louse," modernized rendition.

4. E. Stanley Jones, *Victorious Living*, entry for September 25 (Lucknow, India: Lucknow Publishing House, 1936), 277.

Chapter 4: A Stone for Stumbling

1. Dorothy Sayers, *Letters to a Diminished Church* (Nashville: W Publishing, 2004), 58–59.

2. *Newsweek*, March 1, 1999, 23.

Chapter 5: What Fresh Eyes See

1. Eugene H. Peterson, *The Contemplative Pastor* (Grand Rapids: Eerdmans, 1993), 10.

Chapter 6: Say What?

1. Tom Rees, *Break-Through* (Dallas: Word, 1970), 116–17.
2. Cited by Lisa Miller, "The Age of Divine Disunity: Faith Now Springs from a Hodgepodge of Beliefs," *Wall Street Journal*, February 10, 1999, B-1.
3. "Some Christian Groups Mix Gospel, Aid," *Colorado Springs Gazette*, January 10, 2005.
4. Larry Tomczak, "Crazy Money," *Charisma*, July 2004, 81–86.
5. Rich Nathan, *Who Is My Enemy?* (Grand Rapids: Zondervan, 2002), 10.

Chapter 7: One Lord, One Faith, 31 Flavors

1. Alexis de Tocqueville, *Democracy in America*, ed. Phillips Bradley (New York: Vintage, 1990), 2:106-07.
2. Ibid., 107.
3. Justo L. González, *For the Healing of the Nations* (Maryknoll, N.Y.: Orbis, 1999).
4. John Wesley, "The Character of a Methodist," *The Works of John Wesley*, 3rd ed. (1872; repr., Grand Rapids: Baker, 1991, 1998), 8:339.
5. Charles H. Spurgeon, sermon entitled "The Eternal Name" preached on the evening of May 27, 1855, at Exeter Hall, London. www.spurgeon.org/sermons/0027.htm.
6. Karen Burton Mains, *The Key to a Loving Heart* (Elgin, IL: Cook, 1979), 143–44.

Chapter 8: Consistency, Please

1. Joshua Green, "The Bookie of Virtue," *Washington Monthly*, June 2003.
2. Chuck Colson, "Crown Him Lord of Prime Time," Another Point of View column in Prison Fellowship newsletter.
3. "Marriage and Divorce Rates by State: 1990, 1995, and 1999–2002," Division of Vital Statistics, National Center for Health Statistics, Centers for Disease Control.
4. Dr. Barbara Dafoe Whitehead, interview by Kevin D. Miller, "Ending the Church's Silence on Divorce," *Christianity Today*, November 17, 1999, 53.
5. "Broken Marriages, Not Gay Nuptials, Pose Risk to Kids," *USA Today*, February 24, 2004.
6. See www.emptytomb.org/research.php#Fig1.

Chapter 9: Peace on the Inside

1. Henri J. M. Nouwen, *The Way of the Heart: Desert Spirituality and Contemporary Ministry* (New York: Seabury, 1981).

Chapter 10: Bridge Building

1. Michael Cassidy, *A Witness For Ever* (London: Hodder & Stoughton, 1995), 53.

2. Ibid., 37.

3. Ibid., 180, 183.

4. Ibid., 191–92.

5. As cited by Jones, *Victorious Living*, 344.

6. Ginger Sinsabaugh, *Act Now! Offer Ends Soon!* (Ventura, CA: Regal, 1999), 19.

7. For full information, see the Marriage Savers website (www.marriagesavers. org).

8. See www.arkansas.gov/governor/programs/covenant_marriage.html.

9. Laura Kellams, "Huckabees say 'I do' to Covenant Marriage," *Arkansas Democrat-Gazette* (February 15, 2005).

10. Ibid.

Chapter 11: One-Way Kindness

1. See www.compassion.com.

2. See www.missionofmercy.org.

3. See www.worldvision.org.

4. See www.convoyofhope.org.

5. See www.worldvision.org/loveinc.

Chapter 12: Clearing the Fog

1. Em Griffin, *The Mind Changers* (Wheaton: Tyndale, 1976), 10.

2. Leighton Ford, *Good News Is for Sharing* (Elgin, IL: Cook, 1977), 148.

3. John MacArthur, recorded message at Pastors' Day at the Capitol, May 19, 1999, sponsored by Capitol Ministries, Sacramento, California.

4. Sarah E. Hinlicky, "Talking to Generation X," *First Things*, February 1999, 10–11.

Chapter 13: More Than Words

1. David Pawson, *Word and Spirit Together: Uniting Charismatics and Evangelicals*, 2nd ed. (London: Hodder & Stoughton, 1998), 73.

2. John Wesley, "The Principles of a Methodist, Farther Explained," *The Works of John Wesley*, 3rd ed. (1872; repr. Grand Rapids: Baker, 1991, 1998), 8: 465.

3. Rich Nathan, *Who Is My Enemy? Welcoming People the Church Rejects* (Grand Rapids: Zondervan, 2002), 67–68.

4. Leith Anderson, *A Church for the 21st Century* (Minneapolis: Bethany, 1992), 20.

Chapter 14: Damage Control

1. Nelson D. Lankford, *The Last American Aristocrat* (Boston: Little, Brown, 1996), 224.

Epilogue: Giving Our Best

1. Jones, *Abundant Living*, 183.